THE
HEALTH FOOD DICTIONARY
with Recipes

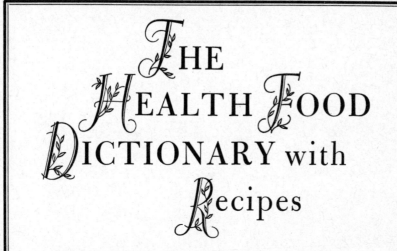

The Health Food Dictionary with Recipes

by

ANSTICE CARROLL

and

EMBREE DE PERSIIS VONA

Illustrated by

Vincenzo De Persiis Vona

Weathervane Books
New York

Design by Janet Anderson

A WARNING This book is *not* for the health food fanatic!

A STATEMENT OF INTENT This book is for the person who browses through a health food store—be it for the first or the hundredth time—and feels overwhelmed or at least slightly confused. And it is also for gourmets who have no intention whatsoever of giving up their croissants and espresso in favor of brewer's yeast or blackstrap molasses, but who would like to *gently ease* a little more health into their lives.

You don't have to completely change your life-style, become a bore on the subject, stop going out to dinner, or drop your unhealthy friends in order to reap the benefits of a more organic way of life. With only a few changes, and delicious ones at that, you can fulfill your wish to eat healthfully and still have delicious food at every meal.

SOME PROBLEMS The health food field is burgeoning, becoming more intricate, and many questions arise. Just what is an organic vegetable—how is it better than its sprayed counterpart; does it taste better; why does it cost more; how can you be sure it's organic; what if it is organic but just doesn't taste as good as what you get at the supermarket? What to do with all those flours—stone ground, pneumatically ground; hard wheat, soft wheat; graham flour, pastry flour—what are the differences between them; what's best for what; can you turn out bread with them that will satisfy your Italian mother-in-law and not only your macrobiotic nephew? Why buy raw milk when your grandmother remembers children dying from unpasteurized milk; can certified raw milk be trusted? What is an organic vitamin; why is it more expensive than its chemical counterpart? What are organic cosmetics; how can you know they are really better than the usual ones, when the labels don't tell you what is in them?

BEFORE YOU BUY . . . READ THIS BOOK How can you avoid getting gypped in a health food store—getting gypped is entirely possible, for opportunists are stumbling all over each other to get a slice of this growing market.

How can you know whether the "raw" sugar you are paying so much for is the real thing or merely refined sugar with a little molasses poured over for coloring to fool you? How can you know whether the "organic" apple juice you are buying is made from unsprayed apples or whether it is just made of ordinary chemical-laden apples processed in a more "organic" manner?

How to answer all the questions? First read this book; you will be placing your feet on firm ground. Then case the local health food outlets. Critically. Ask questions and do not be intimidated by eclectic atmospheres—health food should be for everybody, not just the chosen few. Use this book as a dictionary, to clarify, to verify, to raise questions about what you have seen. Check out store items that seem to be inconsistent with an organic food credo—such as "organic" vitamin pills with artificial coloring, or "pure" vanilla extract containing propylene glycol and other strange things, or instant rose hip tea with artificial sweetening. Ask where the store gets its vegetables, dried fruits, and nuts. Ask if they have been tested for insecticide residues. Visit the farm sources if they are local and you are keen.

By all means, be careful of the word "organic"; everybody is using it and it can mean just about anything, for there are no federal controls exercised over such a label. A fast operator could well chase an organic chicken through his kitchen while the water is boiling, then call the liquid *The Organic Essence of Chicken Broth*—and get away with it! So be careful; and be critical. Your aim is good, healthful, uncontaminated food. Demand it!

AND WE ALSO HAVE RECIPES Now supposing you have found a good dependable health food store. You buy a little whole wheat flour, a little honey, maybe a few nuts. You buy one of the doctrinaire health food cookbooks off the rack. You get home, decide to cook up something healthy, look it up in the book—cookies maybe—and by gosh but aren't there ten ingredients in those almond cookies that you don't have in the kitchen! What to do? Go back to the store and spend a small fortune buying all that strange stuff just to cook up one batch of cookies? *Don't do it!* For here, in this dictionary, you will find simple recipes based around only one or two health food items apiece—the rest of the ingredients you can scrounge out of the most ordinary kitchen (of course, the healthier the better). We will also tell you how to make do with whole wheat flour when a recipe calls for pastry flour; how to substitute honey for sugar and vice versa; how to make flaxseed meal when all you have in the cupboard is flaxseed. Et cetera.

Additional feature: cut down on your stockpile of aspirin and tranquilizers by following our herbal tea hints. Don't believe it? Try it.

Happy reading, shopping, cooking, and eating to you, in the name of health and common sense,

The Authors

For my mother and father

A.C.C.

ACEROLA CHERRY The acerola cherry, also called "Barbados cherry," is a tropical fruit known for its high vitamin C content. In appearance it resembles the common American cherry, but botanically it is not related. Fantastic claims are made for its vitamin C qualities—some scientists maintain that 6 ounces of acerola berries yield as much of the precious vitamin as 50 pounds of fresh cabbage juice (cabbage itself is known for its high vitamin C content). At any rate, that this cherry is far higher than any other known food in natural vitamin C is indisputable.

Acerola berries are often combined with rose hips in vitamin C pills and liquid drops (these are very convenient for infants and young children—and the taste is naturally agreeable).

ACIDOPHILUS MILK This is a cultured milk into which acidophilus bacteria have been introduced. It is not a very stable product, and has to be used within a couple of days of the making. Therefore it is rarely sold commercially. Acidophilus milk aids the growth of healthful intestinal flora and at the same time inhibits the growth of unfriendly bacteria—in much the same manner as yogurt, excepting that the acidophilus is far stronger (and, incidentally, not so appetizing).

In health food stores you will find liquid acidophilus culture and acidophilus food powder. The liquid culture is taken by the teaspoonful or mixed with water or juice. Acidophilus "food" may be taken in conjunction with the culture, and feeds the acidophilus bacteria, making them work more ambitiously.

The culture is also available in pill form, for those who are squeamish about the taste.

ADZUKI BEAN This small dark red bean looks almost too good to eat, more like a polished stone to be treasured than to be treated as a mere dried bean. Dark red is how we usually see it, though straw-colored, brown, and even black adzuki beans are to be found.

The adzuki is imported from Japan, where it is valued highly for its vitamin and mineral content. Those who follow a macrobiotic regimen use it in an endless variety of ways—alone as a vegetable, mixed with rice or other grains, even as pie filling.

The juice derived by boiling the adzuki is said to be beneficial to the kidneys.

Adzuki are delicious as a substitute for black-eyed peas in that mainstay of Southern dishes, the hoppin John. The result is rather more delicate than the original and truly fit for a gourmet's table.

ADZUKI RICE

½ c. adzuki beans	1 c. brown rice
3 c. water	1 tbsp. butter
1½ tsp. salt	

Soak adzuki beans in 1 cup water for 2 hours. Then cook slowly in same liquid for about 1 hour, until slightly tender. Bring 2 cups water to a boil. Add salt. Sprinkle rice into water without disturbing boiling. Add adzuki beans and their liquid. Cover and cook slowly for ¾ hour. Add butter.

Serves four as side dish.

If shorter-cooking rice is used, cook the adzuki beans ½ hour longer before adding to rice. This side dish is also good when served cold. Toss with a little olive oil and garnish with chopped fresh herbs.

AGAR-AGAR Agar-agar, sometimes called Japanese or vegetable gelatin (or just plain agar), comes from a type of seaweed. It is widely used as a thickener and emulsifier by the food processing industry (and among its many other uses finds great service in laboratories as a culture medium). Vegetarians use it to replace common gelatin, which is made from animal protein.

Agar-agar will jell salads and dessert gelatins and thicken soups. When agar-agar is used, fruit and vegetable juices can be jellied merely by warming rather than by boiling, and therefore more of their health value is retained. Jellies and jams made with agar-agar rather than commercial pectin do not need nearly as much sugar or honey (pectin products are very sour and the large amounts of sugar called for are needed more to compensate for this sourness than for that of the fruit). Agar-agar is also useful in cases of constipation, for it swells to many times its bulk when it reaches the intestines and increases peristaltic action without causing painful griping.

Agar-agar comes in flake, granulated, and bar form. These are the basic proportions to use: 3½ cups liquid to 2 tablespoons flakes; 3½ cups liquid to 1 tablespoon granulated; 3½ cups liquid to approximately 7 inches bar form. In all instances, soak the agar-agar in 1 cup of liquid for 10 minutes, then warm on stove until dissolved; add rest of liquid, which should be at room temperature. Refrigerate if desired, but this will jell without refrigeration.

WINE-JELLED PEACHES

7-in. bar agar-agar (see above for proportions of other types agar-agar)
1 c. water

1 4-in. cinnamon stick
2½ c. red wine
½ c. honey (or ¾ c. "raw" sugar)
2 c. sliced fresh peaches

Break agar-agar into pieces and soak in cup of water. Transfer to stove, add cinnamon stick, and heat gently until dissolved (about 20 minutes). Remove from heat, take out cinnamon stick, add wine, honey, and mix well. Refrigerate until semi-jelled. Add sliced peaches and return to refrigerator to complete jelling. This delicious dessert retains a true fresh wine flavor.

Serves six.

ALFALFA The benefits to be derived from this "animal food" should be given their due. Alfalfa is a leguminous plant that has been cultivated for over two thousand years as forage; horses have waxed swift and strong on its healthful properties— and so well might you. The roots of the alfalfa grow extraordinarily deep into the earth and are able to probe out minerals and trace elements that more-shallow-rooted plants cannot reach. Alfalfa is also a rich source of vitamins, including the rare vitamin K, which aids in the normal clotting of blood, and vitamin U, believed to be helpful in the healing of ulcers. Its richness in vitamin A makes it a particularly good food for pregnant and nursing women, and it is said to increase the flow of breast milk.

Chew the leaves raw, add them to salad, or sauté them in oil and serve as a tender vegetable. Gorging yourself on fresh alfalfa would probably not be a good idea, however, for large amounts of the fresh plant have caused various problems in grazing livestock.

Alfalfa is available in health food stores in pill, powder, tea, and seed (for sprouting) form.

ALFALFA LEAF TEA This tea, in addition to its superior nutritive values (see *Alfalfa*), is very easily assimilated and therefore particularly good for the elderly and for children. Its rather bland flavor becomes extremely tasty when mixed with mint. To brew alfalfa tea, steep 1 teaspoon alfalfa leaves in 2 cups boiling water for about 10 minutes.

ALFALFA POWDER Alfalfa leaves can be finely ground into a flourlike powder, which is used as a food supplement. It can be added to a glass of juice or to your bread (½ cup alfalfa powder to 5 cups flour), soups, and stews. Keep in mind, however, that some hay fever sufferers turn out to be allergic to alfalfa hay dust. See also *Alfalfa*.

ALFALFA SEED These tiny seeds produce the tenderest and sweetest of sprouts (see *Sprouts* for simple growing instructions). Alfalfa sprouts are a perfect addition to sandwiches, for they will not go limp after a few hours like lettuce. Add them to salads or put a bowl of them on the table—you may find your children eating them by the handful, for they make an intriguing crunchy snack.

The seeds can be used, unsprouted, for tea—1 teaspoon seeds to 2 cups boiling water. The mild-tasting brew is said to be beneficial in cases of arthritis. See also *Alfalfa*.

ALLSPICE True to its name, allspice tastes like cinnamon, nutmeg, and cloves all combined—if your taste buds can picture that! It is the hard berry of an evergreen tree native to the West Indies. The early Spanish explorers mistook this berry for the peppercorn, which it strongly resembles, and so it also came to

ALLSPICE
Branch–½ size
Fruits–life-size

be known as *pimienta* (Spanish for pepper) and Jamaican pepper. Its pungency enhances the flavor of mincemeat, pickles, and true Italian *mortadella*. The whole berry can be used in marinades, pickles, or broths and gravies (strained). Ground allspice flavors curry and spicy cakes and cookies.

ALMOND   The edible seed of a peachlike tree, the almond is one of the most nutritious of nuts, containing large amounts of protein, vitamin B, calcium, potassium, magnesium, iron, and phosphorus. A few almonds go a long way—this is a highly concentrated food! As a meat substitute, almonds are very useful in vegetarian diets. The brown skin of the raw almond is sometimes irritating to the intestines, and it can be removed by blanching: pour boiling water over the nuts, let them sit for a minute, then slip off the skins—take care not to let the nuts get waterlogged. Ground blanched almonds are the essential ingredient of that European delicacy, marzipan. A milk made from crushed blanched almonds is sometimes recommended for stimulation of milk secretion in nursing mothers, and as an easily digested healthful beverage for babies and children.

There are two varieties of almonds—sweet and bitter. The sweet nuts are the ones we enjoy for their flavor and nutritive value. The bitter almond is utterly unappealing tastewise, and is poisonous as well for it contains prussic acid (also known as hydrogen cyanide and HCN). The bitter almond is used to make almond extract for cooking and oil for skin use; refining removes all trace of poisonous elements.

ALMOND CRESCENTS

1 c. butter
3 tbsp. honey (or ½ c. "raw" sugar)
1 c. ground almonds (blanched or unblanched)

2 c. whole wheat pastry flour
1½ tsp. vanilla

Cream butter. Add honey or sugar, almonds, flour, and vanilla. Mix well, flouring your hands to keep dough from sticking. Shape with fingers into crescent shapes and bake 35 minutes at 300 degrees on a greased cookie sheet. Makes 50 cookies.

6

ALMOND OIL   Almond oil is widely used in the making of cosmetics. In its pure state it is a skin conditioner; it is also good for suntanning and for soothing sunburn. See also *Almond*.

ANISE SEED   The dainty anise plant produces seeds of a most pungent nature. Native to the Near East, from whence it spread to Europe and America, anise seed has for centuries been valued by the cake- and cookie-maker; Romans chased down their feasts with anise cakes that were purported to aid digestion. Anise seed tea (1 teaspoon seeds to 2 cups boiling water), besides its pleasant licorice flavor, claims medicinal qualities for itself as a carminative and a reliever of coughing and asthma. Anise seeds are the essential ingredient of the liqueur *Anisette*, a few drops of which will lend an exotic flair to your demitasse of espresso. Oil of anise is commonly used commercially in cough medicines.

Star anise is the seed of a magnolia-type tree found in southern China, and strangely enough it yields an aroma and oil identical to that of the anise plant. Some connoisseurs claim, however, that the odor of star anise is the more pungent of the two. Certainly star anise is beautiful—the dried pod is shaped like a star, and each of its sections partially encloses one tiny seed. In the Orient it is sometimes regarded as a good luck charm.

Should you have a yen to emulate the gourmets of ancient Rome , try these anise wafers as a fitting finish for a heavy dinner.

ANISE WAFERS

½ c. sugar (preferably "raw" sugar)
3 tsp. anise seed
1 c. butter
1 egg
2 tbsp. brandy (or lemon juice)

2 c. whole wheat flour
1 c. unbleached white flour
1 tsp. baking powder
½ tsp. salt
½ tsp. cinnamon, ground

Put sugar and anise seed in a blender and grind to a powder. Cream sugar-anise powder with the butter. Beat in egg and brandy. Sift in flour, baking powder,

7

salt, and cinnamon. Mix well. Shape into a ball, wrap in wax paper or plastic, and chill for 30 minutes. Roll out on a floured board to ⅛-inch thickness. Cut into shapes with cooky cutters. Place on an oiled cookie sheet and bake in a 350-degree oven for about 12 minutes, or until brown. Makes about 60 cookies.

APPLE, DRIED The dried apple is moist and nonsticky —a neat snack for children. It is not a particularly low-calorie food; however, its calories will work for, not against, you, because dried apples contain many valuable nutrients.

Dried apples can be soaked in water overnight and substituted with fairly good results in recipes that call for fresh apples. Stewed, with a little honey and lemon juice added, they rest on their own merits. This is the most yang of fruits in the macrobiotic scale and is widely used by those who follow such a regimen.

APRICOT, DRIED The apricot tree first gave fruit in Armenia and the mountainous regions of Asia; now, several thousand years later, it is grown in temperate climates throughout the world. Its dried fruit is a valuable source of vitamin A and also contains healthy amounts of potassium, niacin, sodium, magnesium, and iron—a very useful item! If you stew apricots or soak them overnight, they act as a mild purgative.

Avoid dried apricots whose color is too brilliant—they have probably been treated with sulphur. Those of more muted tones may not be as eye-catching, but they are usually tastier and far more healthful.

APRICOT CAKE

1 c. dried apricots (un-sulphured)
1 c. water
2 c. sugar (preferably "raw" sugar)
¼ lb. plus 2 tbsp. butter
1 tsp. vanilla extract

1½ tsp. grated lemon peel (organic undyed lemon, if possible)
2 eggs
2 c. whole wheat pastry flour
½ tsp. salt
2¼ tsp. baking powder
1 c. milk

Soak apricots in water for about 2 hours. Add ½ cup sugar and 2 tablespoons butter and simmer gently until sugar and butter dissolve. Put mixture through blender or food mill. Set aside.

Cream remaining butter and sugar. Add vanilla, lemon peel, and eggs one at a time, stirring well.

Add sifted flour, salt, and baking powder alternately with milk and beat until smooth, but do not overbeat. Pour batter into an 8-inch springform pan. Spread apricot puree gently over top of batter, slightly thinner toward the middle. Bake at 350 degrees for about 1 hour, until cake pulls away from sides of pan.

During baking, the apricot puree will penetrate the cake and end up in a layer at the bottom. Top each piece with a dollop of whipped cream, or leave as is—delicious either way.

APRICOT KERNEL These bitter kernels look like unblanched almonds. They are sold in some health food stores because of their laetril content, which may be beneficial in the treatment of certain types of cancer. Approach them with *extreme* caution: apricot kernels contain amygdalin which can be converted by the body into cyanide—a lethal poison.

APRICOT KERNEL OIL This oil is used primarily as a cosmetic item. The hundred-year-old ladies of Hunza are said to owe their wrinkle-free complexions to apricot kernel oil.

ARAMI This Japanese seaweed is a slightly larger form of hiziki (see *Hiziki*).

ARROWROOT STARCH Arrowroot starch is a fine white substance that is known variously as arrowroot starch, arrowroot flour, and arrowroot powder. The arrowroot plant is a tropical perennial herb whose food value lies in its starchy rootlike rhizomes. The starch of the arrowroot is of a very fine grain—much finer than potato starch; it is thus easily digestible and suitable for invalid and infant diets (for this purpose, make a smooth paste of the arrowroot, add warm milk or water, and

9

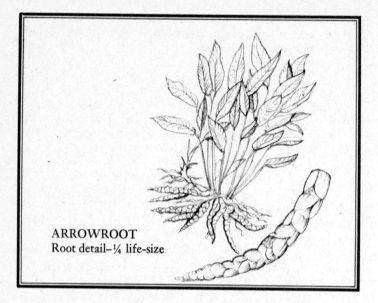

ARROWROOT
Root detail—¼ life-size

honey to taste). Arrowroot starch can be used to thicken gravies, soups, and fruit compotes in the same manner as cornstarch.

ARTICHOKE NOODLE The light and tasty artichoke noodle is made from the flour of the Jerusalem artichoke, a tuber-bearing type of sunflower that was native to North America before being introduced into Europe in the seventeenth century. The unlikely name (for it is neither from Jerusalem nor in the least resembles an artichoke) seems to have derived in part from the Spanish word for "sunflower," *girasole;* as for "artichoke," its derivation is a mystery! The tuber, which looks somewhat like a small potato, is rich in iron and inulin, a sugar that can be eaten by diabetics. Jerusalem artichoke noodles also have a far lower carbohydrate content than noodles made of hard wheat.

AVOCADO OIL An ingredient in cosmetics, this pure fruit oil is also sold as a salad or cooking oil. It is most often mixed with other vegetable oils—used alone it would be like pouring liquid gold on your lettuce, for it is an expensive item. For use as a cosmetic, you will save money by buying the edible oil, instead of an expensive cosmetic preparation. Considered one of the most penetrating of all oils, it is a marvelous skin softener.

BAKING POWDER Baking powder is used as a leavening agent in cookies and quick breads, but it can be a very dangerous product. Most commercial brands contain aluminum compounds, which should not be used for human consumption. Less objectionable, but nevertheless harmful for many people, is the high sodium content of many baking powders. So if you want to use this product, check your labels carefully. Health food stores generally carry low sodium, aluminum-free brands of baking powder.

BALM The lemon-scented balm leaf holds a time-honored position in medicinal and culinary circles. Balm tea, which is also known as lemon balm and Melissa tea (from its botanical name *Melissa officinalis*), has a delicate lemon-mint flavor and is valued as a carminative and a reducer of fever. Use 1 teaspoon of dried leaves to 2 cups of boiling water. Balm tea has value as a nerve soother, and an Arabian proverb goes even further: Balm tea "makes the heart merry and joyful!" If you plan on living a hundred years, this gentle tea might help you reach your goal, for legend tells that balm wards off old age.

Fresh or dried balm will impart a delicious lemony flavor to fish, lamb, and poultry stuffing; or sprinkle it on your salad.

BANANA, DRIED The banana is the fruit of a giant tropical herb that can grow to a height of 30 feet. After each harvest the "tree" dies and its roots send up another enormous shoot. When unripe, the banana is a very starchy food, and a nutritious, easily digested flour is made from it; this is rarely exported. As the fruit ripens, black specks appear on its surface, indicating that the starch is turning to sugar—from which point the banana is deliciously edible. The more unripe the banana, the more constipating it is; the more ripe, the more laxative it becomes.

The ripe fruit can be dried to produce a compact energy-giving food that is extremely rich in potassium and magnesium. It is also high in calories; these are not empty calories, however, but are full of nutrients. Dried banana flakes are also available, and these can be sprinkled on cereal or yogurt dishes.

BANCHA TWIG TEA This is Japanese green tea (see *Tea, Oriental*) made from tea leaves that have been aged three years on the tree—hence its brown color. Bancha twig tea is the everyday beverage of the macrobiotic. Roast in a heavy skillet until an aroma arises. The tea can then be stored in a tightly sealed jar and used as needed. Add a generous pinch of roasted bancha tea to a quart of water (use an enamel pot or pan) and boil gently for 20 minutes; strain and serve. When a dash of soy sauce is added, this makes a very bracing, strengthening tea.

BARLEY, PEARLED To produce pearled barley, the bran is removed from the barley grain. This is an inferior product, healthwise, to the whole hulled variety, and is best used in times of illness when other foods cannot be tolerated. It is the mildest and least irritating of cereal foods.

BARLEY, WHOLE HULLED Pliny wrote in Roman times that barley was the oldest cultivated grain. Modern investigation tends to bear out his opinion; deposits of barley have been found in Stone Age lake dwellings in Switzerland. An extremely hardy grain that can withstand extremes of temperature, barley is grown as far north as the Arctic Circle and flourishes in subtropical countries as well. Barley malt has been used since prehistoric times in the making of beer.

Whole hulled barley is the most nutritious form of this grain, for it still bears its bran coating, which is high in B vitamins. Barley is most delicious when added to stews and soups; it lends a satisfying creamy texture. See also *Barley, Pearled*.

BARLEY-BEEF SOUP

2 lb. short ribs of beef,
    cut in 3-in. pieces
2½ qt. water
¾ c. barley, whole hulled
2 bay leaves
Salt and pepper to taste

1 c. each of any 4
    chopped fresh vege-
    tables, such as:
    onions
    carrots
    celery
    green beans
    tomatoes, peeled and
      seeded
    zucchini, etc.

Simmer short ribs in water for 3 hours until just tender. If you do this the day before serving, refrigerate the pot overnight, then skim off congealed fat and continue soup. If you prepare the beef the morning before serving, put in freezer for 1–2 hours, and fat will rise enough for thorough skimming.

Put soup back on stove. Add washed barley, bay leaves, salt, and pepper and simmer 1 hour. Meanwhile chop fresh vegetables; add and simmer ½ hour more, until everything is tender. Taste for seasoning.

Serves six.

BARLEY FLOUR   The best barley flour is ground from whole hulled barley. When added to bread recipes, barley flour gives a moist, cakelike texture. The barley-orange bread below is useful for the allergy prone, for it is wheat- and milk-free—and also tastes good.

BARLEY-ORANGE BREAD

2 eggs, well beaten
½ c. fresh-squeezed
    orange juice
2 tbsp. oil (preferably
    pressed oil)
½ c. honey
½ c. water

¼ c. grated orange peel
    (from organic undyed
    oranges)
2 c. barley flour
⅔ c. sugar (preferably
    "raw" sugar)
½ tsp. salt
3 tsp. baking powder

Mix together beaten eggs, orange juice, oil, honey, water, and grated orange peel. Sift together flour, sugar, salt, and baking powder. Stir wet mixture into dry, beating well. Pour into well-oiled and floured bread pan. Bake at 350 degrees for about 70 minutes.

This is a moist, sweet bread, perfect for tea or dessert.

BARLEY GRITS Coarsely ground whole barley forms a type of grits that is quickly cooked and particularly good as a morning cereal.

BASIL This aromatic herb is surely a god's gift to the kitchen; and divine favor shines brilliantly upon the Mediterranean's sunny shores where basil has long grown in great profusion. The name "basil" comes from the Greek word for "king"—so greatly did the Greeks esteem this king of herbs. *Herbe royale*, the French respectfully call it. In Italy basil serves the goddess Love; a sprig of it worn by a suitor bespeaks his loving intentions. In India, too, the herb flourishes freely and is held in reverence by the Hindus who plant it to protect both the living and the dead. Basil can also prosper in your own summer garden or flowerpot!

In fresh or dried form, basil will lend savory flavoring to tomato dishes, soups, ragouts, sauces, sausages, and salads. The pungency of basil, unlike most other herbs, increases with cooking, so handle it with care until you learn to know it well. Basil tea makes a delicious drink, hot or cold; brew it from fresh or dried leaves, a heaping teaspoon per cup, and steep for 15 minutes.

The leaves of basil are said to be antiseptic; either the fresh leaf or a decoction of the dried leaf is soothing to insect bites and stings.

TOMATOES STUFFED WITH
BASIL AND RICE

4 good-sized firm tomatoes	2 tbsp. chopped fresh or 1 tbsp. dried parsley
1 c. cooked rice (preferably brown rice)	2 finely chopped cloves of garlic
2 tbsp. chopped fresh or 1 tbsp. dried basil	1½ tsp. olive oil (preferably pressed oil)
	1 tsp. salt

Cut a lid off the top of each tomato and scoop out the inside pulp, taking care not to weaken the walls. Chop the tomato pulp and mix with the other ingredients.

Stuff the tomatoes with the mixture, put tomato tops
back on as lids, and place in an uncovered baking dish.
Bake at 350 degrees for about ½ hour.

These tomatoes can be served hot but are particularly
delicious cold, and their flavor blossoms after a day or
so of refrigeration.

PESTO ALLA GENOVESE

*36 leaves fresh basil (or 2
    tbsp. dried)
1 garlic clove
1 handful pignoli nuts
    (or walnuts)*

*2 tbsp. grated Parmesan
    cheese
½ tsp. salt
½ tsp. black pepper,
    freshly ground
⅔ c. olive oil (preferably
    pressed oil)*

Finely chop basil, garlic, and nuts (or pulverize in
mortar). Put in a small bowl, stir in Parmesan, next salt
and pepper, then oil. (Or put all ingredients into a
blender, but the sauce will lose some texture.) This
pesto is a superb sauce for spaghetti (enough for 1
pound). It can also be added to vegetable or bean soups
with most appetizing results.

BAY LEAF   The bay laurel tree is actually a large evergreen shrub. Its history is a lengthy and noble one; among the
ancient Greeks the laurel tree was sacred to the god Apollo. A
wreath of its branches became the symbol of victory—in war,
athletic games, and literary contests—and today we still have
our poet laureates. Legend has it that lightning will never strike
a bay laurel tree, and the emperor Tiberius is said to have worn
a laurel wreath on his head during thunderstorms. Well—it
wouldn't hurt to try!

Bay leaves are very pungent in the cooking pot, so be stingy
with them. One leaf will lend its characteristic bitter taste to a
stew or soup for four people. Remove the leaf before serving,
because no amount of cooking will render it tender enough
to eat.

Use a bay leaf in your marinade, or when boiling tongue, or
preparing fish stock. And of course the crumbled bay leaf is
essential to a bouquet garni.

BEANS, DRIED Dried beans are available to us in a most fantastic variety—fava beans, pinto beans, kidney beans, mung beans, soy beans, marrow beans, split yellow peas, split green peas, whole peas, cowpeas, chick-peas, adzuki beans. The list could go on and on. Beans offer an extremely good source of protein, niacin, vitamins B_1 and B_2, as well as valuable minerals such as iron, magnesium, sodium, and calcium. Their protein content makes them an excellent meat substitute. With a dozen glass jars of different beans (for why not display their beauty rather than tuck them away in a dark cupboard) in your kitchen, you will be able to give any one basic recipe twelve completely different faces. And dried beans are cheap! Organically grown ones less so than the chemically grown, of course, but their superior flavor usually makes the additional expense worthwhile.

Tips on cooking dried beans: With the exception of split peas and lentils, all beans should be soaked overnight before cooking. Or instead of long soaking, bring beans and water to a rolling boil, then turn off heat and soak for two hours; use as needed. One cupful of dried beans will swell in bulk to feed about four people. Cook beans slowly so that they do not burst and lose their shape. Slow cooking also cuts down on the gas-producing tendencies of dried beans.

See also individual beans.

BEAN SOUP

1 c. white beans, dried
  (or kidney beans,
  fava beans, pinto
  beans, chick-peas,
  etc.)
3 qt. water (or vegetable
  or meat broth)
Optional: ham bone, or ½
  lb. diced salt pork or
  prosciutto ends
1 bay leaf
3 tbsp. olive oil (preferably pressed oil)

8 cups any assorted fresh
  vegetables on hand:
  chopped onions
  sliced carrots
  sliced zucchini
  diced eggplant
  diced string beans
  diced tomatoes
  peas, etc.
1 c. macaroni (preferably
  soy, whole wheat, or
  buckwheat)
Salt and pepper to taste
2 tbsp. chopped parsley

17

Soak beans in 1 quart water overnight. Do not throw out the soaking water. Add another 2 quarts water or broth, bone or meat if you use it, bay leaf, and simmer slowly until beans are almost tender (about 3 hours). Sauté freshly chopped vegetables in oil and add to soup. Add macaroni, salt, and pepper, and simmer about ½ hour until everything is tender. Add parsley and serve. Or let the soup stand for a few hours before serving; its taste will be even fuller.

Serves four to six.

BEARBERRY TEA   This bitter tea from the dried leaves of a trailing evergreen shrub (*Arctostaphylos uva-ursi*) has long been used in cases of bladder inflammation and kidney disease. It is soothing and increases the flow of urine. It contains tannic acid. Steep 1 teaspoon dried bearberry leaves in 2 cups boiling water for 20 minutes.

BLACK COHOSH TEA   Also known as rattlesnake or squawroot, this perennial herb (*Cimicifuga racemosa*) is native to the United States. Hearsay has it that the root contains an antidote for rattlesnake poison. The tea, however, is used as a sedative for hysteria and spasmodic diseases and is said to be useful in easing childbirth, asthma, whooping cough, and kidney problems—quite a catchall!

To brew the tea, steep 1 teaspoonful of the chopped dried root in 1 cup boiling water for 15 minutes.

BLACKSTRAP MOLASSES   See *Molasses.*

BLADDER WRACK TEA   Bladder wrack is a seaweed that grows attached to rocks rather than to the sea bottom. Its tea is rich in iodine and trace minerals. Steep 1 teaspoon bladder wrack in 2 cups boiling water for 15 minutes.

BLUEBERRY TEA   This tea is made from the dried crushed leaves of the blueberry bush. When taken regularly and over a long period of time it is said to be an effective remedy for diabetes. Steep 1 teaspoon dried leaves in 2 cups boiling water for 20 minutes.

B R A N   Bran is the outer coating of the wheat kernel; in it are concentrated valuable amounts of minerals and vitamin B. In the making of commercial flours and breads, the bran is almost always removed—in honor of pure whiteness.

There are problems with bran, however. Pesticides are said to be strongly concentrated in the bran layer of the wheat kernel. Therefore, take care that your whole wheat flour is organically grown. Certain people with peptic ulcers or intestinal problems find bran difficult to tolerate. There is a way around this: when making your whole wheat bread, mix everything except the yeast, keeping the mixture rather moist, and let it stand overnight; in the morning add the yeast dissolved in a little water, and knead well, using unbleached white flour for dusting. You will find that this method also overcomes problems of dryness and crumbling in the bread.

Bran is sometimes recommended as a laxative. Be careful, however, for bran can be an intestinal irritant unless properly soaked or cooked.

B R A Z I L   N U T   The brazil nut is the fruit of a tall South American tree. Each of its large woody fruits carries a dozen to two dozen nuts inside, arranged like the sections of an orange. The individual nuts also have a very hard covering—as anyone who has struggled to crack one can vouch. Brazil nuts are high in phosphorus, protein, and unsaturated oils. They are a concentrated nutrient and should be eaten sparingly and chewed well. Delicious nut butter can be made by grinding the brazil nut either alone or with cashew nuts; like all pure nut butters, this should be kept refrigerated.

B R E A D   In Roman times, whiteness of bread carried an "upper-class" connotation; dark bread was the fare of the common people. For in those days it was far easier simply to use whole ground wheat kernel for bread than to sift and bolt and

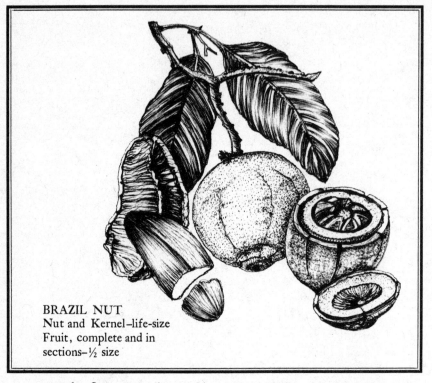

BRAZIL NUT
Nut and Kernel–life-size
Fruit, complete and in
sections–½ size

age the flour to attain a whiter color. Today, however, the
tables have turned! It is now far easier and cheaper to produce
lily-white bread than whole grain bread. The white bread of
the rich has become the food of the people, and the dark loaf of
the poor graces the tables of the well-to-do.

Expect bread made from stone-ground organically grown
wheat to be expensive. The fact that the flour is stone ground,
that it is grown without pesticides, that it contains the germ
and bran of the kernel, and that it has not been bleached adds
to the expense. And all these essentials that make whole bread
healthful and delectable are anathema to the industrialized food
field.

Consider by contrast the manner in which bread flour is
treated by the food moguls. First the grain is grown on chemically fertilized and pesticide-laden soils; next it is robbed of
bran and germ, taking away its very essence and leaving pri-

marily starch; then it is pulverized in grinding machines that reach such degrees of heat, the resulting flour is actually "precooked" (with corresponding loss of nutrients). Finally the flour, if it can now be called so, is bleached with chlorine dioxide (a poison). This wondrous white powder is now prepared to sit for any number of years on the grocer's shelf—no fear that it will spoil or bugs will touch it—or it is made into loaves of spongy tastelessness, shot with emulsifiers to imitate eggs and cream, with dye to imitate whole wheat, with mold inhibitors, hydrogenated fats, and synthetic vitamins in a vain attempt to resuscitate a dead subject.

By giving up white "commercial" bread, you need not be doomed forever to the leaden loaves (nonetheless delightful to the appreciative taste) of the intrepid macrobiotic. Not at all! If your nearest "natural" bakery or health food store cannot satisfy your desire for a buoyant loaf that will not overpower the food that accompanies it, become a baker yourself. It is a joyous activity, and if your experimentations don't at first reach your ideal, at least they'll make the most delicious rejects going. By juggling the amounts of whole wheat flour, whole wheat pastry flour, unbleached white flour, etc., you will be able to achieve loaves as heavy or as light, as strong-flavored or as subtle-tasting, as you desire.

Bread crumbs (toss a few slices of bread in the blender and *voilà!*) and bread dishes take on an extra dimension when made with whole grain bread. Try the easy "soufflé" below and you will see.

GOLDEN CHEESE "SOUFFLE"

2 eggs
2 c. milk (part of this can
    be cream, if extra
    richness is desired)
½ tsp. salt
½ tsp. paprika
½ tsp. dry mustard
3 tsp. minced onion

2 tbsp. melted butter
6 slices whole grain bread
    (or more, if needed)
¼ lb. grated cheddar
    cheese
¼ lb. grated Parmesan
    cheese

Beat together eggs, milk, salt, paprika, mustard, and onion. Put melted butter in bottom of a shallow baking dish. Arrange alternating layers of sliced bread, mixed grated cheeses, and egg mixture, ending with grated cheese on top. Bake 45 minutes at 325 degrees.

Serves four.

BREWER'S YEAST This yeast was originally a by-product of the brewing industry—hence its name. Today, however, it is grown specifically for human consumption and is a rich source of vitamin B, containing all the elements of the B complex and a large amount of protein. Great for instant pep and sustained energy, it is a boon to those who watch their weight, for it contains little fat, carbohydrates, or sugar—it will not of itself make you lose weight, but will give you the energy to zip off unwanted poundage. If you are deficient in the B vitamins, you may find that brewer's yeast at first produces gas, therefore work up to a good dosage gradually, starting with a teaspoonful or less. Shop around for a brand of yeast that is palatable to you; if you can't stomach one kind, give it to your pets (in small amounts) and try again!

Brewer's yeast comes in powder, flake, and pill form. The flakes dissolve more easily than the powder, and the pills are convenient for travelers, but the powder is far more concentrated than either and offers an immediate pickup too good to be missed. Try it in the high-energy drinks below.

Brewer's yeast can also be added in small amounts to breads, soups, stews, meat loafs, etc. A caution: Do not confuse this yeast, whose growth has been arrested by heating, with baking yeast, which is a live substance that may continue growing in the intestines with deleterious results.

VANILLA YEAST SHAKE

2 c. milk
1 tbsp. brewer's yeast
    powder

½ tsp. vanilla extract
2 tbsp. honey

Blend all together.

BANANA YEAST SHAKE

2 c. milk
1 tbsp. brewer's yeast
   powder

½ fresh banana
2 tsp. honey (optional)

Blend all together.

PAPAYA YEAST DRINK

1 c. diced papaya (a
   properly ripe papaya
   should be very soft on
   the outside)

1½ c. apple juice
½ banana (optional)
1 tsp. honey
1 tbsp. brewer's yeast
   powder

Blend all together.

BUCHU LEAF TEA The buchu plant is native to South Africa and has not been successfully grown elsewhere. It is, however, imported, and tea made from steeping 1 teaspoon buchu leaves in 1 cup boiling water for about 30 minutes is said to be good for bladder and kidney diseases.

BUCKTHORN BARK TEA This tea, prepared from the dried and seasoned bark of the Alder Buckthorn (*Rhamnus frangula*), is mildly laxative and has the advantage of not being habit forming.

To brew, use 1 teaspoon of buckthorn to each cup of boiling water; steep 2 to 4 minutes.

BUCKWHEAT A hardy grasslike herb, buckwheat produces a three-cornered seed, known as kasha or buckwheat groats, that is used in much the same manner as grain. High in potassium and phosphorus, it is considered the most yang of cereals by the macrobiotics. Buckwheat is a staple in Russia and in Brittany, but it is not so commonly used in the United States. That is unfortunate, for buckwheat is one of the few commercially grown products that is not routinely doused with insecticides—for its extreme hardiness makes it almost blight-free. Buckwheat is grown extensively for honey-making; dark and flavorful, it yields one of the most nutritious of honeys.

Buckwheat groats are generally available roasted or raw. If you enjoy a really fresh-roasted flavor, buy the raw groats and roast them yourself; just put them in a heavy frying pan over medium heat and stir until browned on all sides. Kasha (as buckwheat groats are more usually called) can be served as a warming breakfast cereal, with honey and cream added. It can also be used as stuffing for game or fowl, or served as a rice substitute. If you find the pungent musty flavor of kasha a little strange at first, try mixing it with rice (see recipe below).

KASHA WITH RICE

4 c. water	1 egg
1½ tsp. salt	1 c. kasha (roasted)
1 c. brown rice	1 tbsp. butter

Bring salted water to boil. Meanwhile wash brown rice in a sieve and drain it. When water reaches rolling boil, sprinkle rice in slowly enough so that the water does not stop boiling. Cover tightly.
Beat egg and mix with kasha until all grains are coated. In a hot heavy frying pan stir this mixture briskly until each grain of kasha is dry and separate. When rice has been cooking for 15 minutes, add the kasha to it and cover. Cook for ½ hour more, until liquid is absorbed and kasha and rice are tender. Add butter.
Serves four.

BUCKWHEAT FLOUR This gray flour speckled with black is traditionally used in the United States for the making of buckwheat pancakes. Their Russian counterpart—blini—is not limited to the breakfast table; served with red caviar and sour cream, they render any meal exotic. Buckwheat flour can also be added to bread recipes in small amounts (approximately ½ cup buckwheat flour to 4 cups wheat flour).

Commercially milled buckwheat flour usually finds its way into pancake mixes; it is rarely sold as is. Best to purchase this flour stone ground from a miller or health food store. See also *Buckwheat*.

BLINI (BUCKWHEAT PANCAKES)

1 c. milk
½ c. water
2 tbsp. pressed vegetable
    oil or melted butter
2 tbsp. honey
1 egg

½ c. buckwheat flour
½ c. whole wheat pastry
    flour
2 tsp. baking powder
½ tsp. salt

Beat together milk, water, oil, honey, and egg. Sift dry ingredients into liquid mixture and stir just enough to dampen the flour; do not overbeat. The batter should be rather thin.
To cook, lightly oil a cast-iron griddle or heavy frying pan. Heat until drops of water sprinkled on it dance. Spoon batter onto griddle; cook until bubbly on top, then turn over and brown the other side. Try not to turn more than once. Serve hot with butter and maple syrup; or with butter, sour cream, and red caviar. Makes 21 six-inch blini.

BUCKWHEAT GRITS Coarsely ground buckwheat grits make an ideal winter cereal and are quicker cooking than the whole groats. See also *Buckwheat*.

BUCKWHEAT GROATS See *Buckwheat*.

BULGUR Bulgur is to the Middle East what rice is to the Orient and kasha is to Russia. It is a cracked wheat that retains the bran and germ of the grain. In olden times it was roasted in open braziers, dried in the sun, then cracked in mortar and pestle. Today the methods have been mechanized but the basic process remains the same.

Bulgur is a most versatile grain and very simple to prepare. Everything from salads to cereals takes on new interest when bulgur is used.

25

BULGUR

1 *medium-size onion,* *sliced thin*	1 *c. bulgur*
2 *tbsp. vegetable oil* *(preferably pressed* *oil)*	2 *c. chicken or vegetable* *broth (or water)*
	1 *tsp. salt*

Gently sauté onion in oil for about 3 minutes. Add bulgur and stir to coat all grains with oil. Add broth, salt, and bring to a boil. Cover and turn heat down to simmering. Cook about 20 minutes or until liquid is absorbed and bulgur is fluffy. Serves 4 people as a substitute for rice or potatoes.

TABOOLEY
(BULGUR AND PARSLEY SALAD)

¾ *c. bulgur*	*Italian parsley (or*
1 *c. boiling water*	½ *c. dried)*
1 *clove garlic, finely* *chopped*	3 *chopped tomatoes*
	1 *tsp. salt*
½ *c. fresh mint, finely* *chopped (or 2 tbsp.* *dried)*	½ *tsp. pepper*
	½ *c. lemon juice*
1½ *c. chopped fresh*	½ *c. olive oil (preferably* *pressed oil)*

Soak bulgur in 1 cup boiling water for ½ hour or until water is absorbed. Mix in chopped ingredients, then add salt and pepper, lemon juice, and olive oil.

Serves four.

BURDOCK In Japan and Hawaii the importance of burdock root (also known as gobo) is well appreciated and the plant is extensively cultivated. In the United States burdock (*Arctium lappa*) is regarded as an all too common and pesky weed. If you do not come across this large-leafed plant in your backyard, go to an Oriental or macrobiotic market. There you will be sure to find the long skinny burdock root, which is a common ingredient of nituke—sautéed vegetables Japanese style. The tender young stems of burdock may also be eaten—peeled and steamed and served with butter, yielding a delicious vegetable much like asparagus.

Tea prepared from either the root or the seed of the burdock is said to be an extremely effective blood purifier. As such it is reputedly helpful in remedying skin disorders and rheumatic pains. Steep 1 teaspoon dried root in 1 cup boiling water for 5 minutes. Strain and serve with honey if desired.

BURNET The cucumberlike flavor of this herb will enhance any salad; in fact it is often known as salad burnet. It will also add a spark to iced drinks and creamed vegetable dishes. The tea made from its dried leaves is useful as a cleansing tonic; it also has certain antiseptic qualities, is soothing when applied to skin wounds, and is said to stem the flow of blood. To brew burnet tea, steep 1 teaspoon dried leaves in 2 cups boiling water for about 15 minutes.

BUTTER If you can find a source of natural untampered-with butter, you truly have a treasure. For the taste of *real* butter is all but lost to us. Industrialized butter production has seen to that. The commercial butter you buy can be bleached, dyed, made from stale cream with rancidity disguised by additives and preservatives, and enormously oversalted. Many people recommend the use of unsalted butter on the grounds that it contains fewer additives—for there is no salt to disguise the chemical flavors. However, if you try making your own butter (simple instructions below), you will see how truly far even commercial sweet butter is from the taste of real butter.

How to deal with the problem: Buy "organic" butter, if you can find it—and afford it. Or make your own . . . also an expensive proposition because of the high price of heavy cream, but definitely worth it to complement a special loaf of bread. Otherwise the best you can do is buy genuinely sweet cream butter from as reputable a dairy as you can find.

BUTTER IN THE BLENDER

½ pt. *heavy cream*   ½ c. *ice water*

Whip cream in blender at high speed. When whipped, add ice water and continue at high speed until butter is formed (this can take a minute or two). Pour butter into sieve to drain. Makes about ½ cup butter. Do not throw away the drippings; use them in cooking.
Butter can also be made in the same manner in an electric mixer.

BUTTERMILK In foregone times, buttermilk was the natural by-product of butter-making. As cream was churned, butter separated from it, leaving a thick low-fat acidulous milk flecked with bits of butter. This was drained off by removing a plug from the bottom of the churn.

Today's buttermilk usually has nothing to do with butter. It is an imitation of what used to be, and is made from skim milk with culture added to give acidity, and flecks of butter thrown in for nostalgia's sake—the "churning" alluded to on the label often refers merely to the mixing of these extraneous bits of butter into the skim milk. It is a healthful product, low in fat, high in calcium—but it is not buttermilk! Certified raw buttermilk is to be preferred over the pasteurized kind—if you can find it.

Buttermilk is often recommended for pregnant and nursing women, for while being low in fat, at the same time it provides the acid and enough fat to increase absorption of much-needed calcium, and is high in B vitamins.

 CANDY, HEALTH FOOD Read the labels on so-called health food candy with care. Often the names of these items will lead you to believe that they are healthful and nutritious, when they are only fattening and destructive—with fine print revealing questionable ingredients such as sugar, corn syrup, dextrose, cottonseed oil, and even chocolate. Buy carefully . . . and then enjoy.

CANE SYRUP Cane syrup, a by-product of sugar refining, is a thick, dark golden syrup containing more sugar than molasses. It is used primarily in the southern United States, in the same manner as maple syrup is used in the north. "Organically" refined cane syrup has not been treated with the usual lime or sulphur.

CARAWAY SEED The fruit of the caraway herb is commonly called a seed. Caraway is native to Europe, Siberia, and the Himalayas; it is said that the farther north it grows, the more aromatic are the seeds. As a medicinal, 1 teaspoon bruised seeds to 2 cups boiling water gives a tea that is valued as a digestive and expeller of gas. In cooking it is used to flavor bread, cakes and cookies, sauerkraut, and mild cheeses. Next time you serve bread and any Muenster-type cheese, put a small bowl of caraway seeds on the table; sprinkled on a slice of cheese they add delicious pungency and aroma. Caraway is also the flavor base of Kümmel liqueur.

CARDAMOM SEED Cardamom pods, the fruit of a herbacious plant native to India and Ceylon, contain aromatic seeds that are used to flavor desserts, mulled wines, and curries. They must be harvested carefully lest the pod split open and the seeds lose some of their heady essence. In the Orient cardamom seeds are chewed to sweeten the breath; early American colonists used them for the same purpose.

CAROB POD The flat leathery seed pods of the carob tree are sometimes called St. John's bread in reference to a belief that these pods were the "locust" St. John fed on in the wilderness—for the honey locust tree is somewhat similar to the carob tree. The carob tree is native to the Mediterranean region; before chocolate became a common commodity, the dry carob pod was a "candy" to the poorer children of that area. Chewing carob pods may not appeal to more refined tastes, but they do yield a sugary, vaguely chocolatelike flavor and lots of nutrients in the form of minerals and vitamin A.

Carob is used nowadays mainly as a chocolate substitute for those who are allergic to chocolate or wish to avoid it because of its high fat content (carob has 2 percent fat as opposed to the 52 percent in chocolate). Carob can yield some delicious confections, but don't expect them to taste just like chocolate or you are doomed to disappointment.

CAROB POWDER The flourlike powder of the ground carob is found toasted and raw. The toasted powder is a dark brown, similar in appearance to cocoa, and this is mostly used as a chocolate substitute. As a general rule, 3 teaspoons carob powder plus 2 tablespoons liquid (water or milk) equal 1 square of unsweetened chocolate.

CARRAGEEN See *Irish Moss*.

CASHEW NUT The cashew nut is actually the seed of the cashew fruit, a fleshy pear-shaped "apple." The seed grows in a curious manner—it hangs, kidney-shaped, from the outside

CASHEW NUT
Kernel–life-size
Branch with fruits–⅔ size

end of the fruit. The tree is native to tropical countries, Kashmir being one of the most important producers. The cashew "apple" is used locally as a fruit and to make a fermented liquor called *kajú*. The tree is related to the poison sumac, and the shells of the nuts contain an oil that is extremely irritating to the skin. The hull of the cashew nut and the poison juices are removed by roasting, leaving the pale soft delectable nut that graces our tables.

High in unsaturated fats and protein, the cashew nut also supplies good amounts of magnesium, sodium, and iron. It is an extremely versatile nut. Because of its softness it can easily be blended to a smooth paste and used in cream soups, milk, ice cream, and nut butter. And, of course, cashew nuts are unbeatable *au naturel*.

CATNIP Cats should not be given the monopoly on this useful herb. A member of the mint family, the leaves of the catnip yield a pleasing and useful tea. It was much appreciated in England before the introduction of Oriental teas and was also used by the American Indians. It is therapeutic as an inducer of perspiration in cases of fever, as a carminative, and as a relaxant and sleep inducer. Catnip tea is said to work wonders with colicky infants; it is soothing and quieting and may save mothers some sleepless nights. For you or your child, steep 1 teaspoon dried or fresh crushed catnip leaves in 2 cups boiling water, and reap the calming benefits.

CAYENNE PEPPER This red spice comes from bushy tropical pepper plants of the genus *Capsicum*—a completely different species from the black-pepper-producing vine *Piper nigrum*. Extremely useful as a stimulant, it gives tone to the circulation and heals lacerations. It will even warm your feet if you sprinkle a little on the bottom of your socks!

Add cayenne to any dish that needs a lift—fish sauce, cream soup, eggs, cheese dishes. Remember that heat brings out the hot flavor, so stir a little before you taste. Cayenne differs in degree of hotness, depending on the source; certain imported types are generally more potent than domestic brands.

WELSH RAREBIT

3 tbsp. butter	*½ c. beer*
1 lb. cheddar cheese	*¼ tsp. dry mustard*
(sharp or mild, or	*⅛ tsp. cayenne pepper*
combination of the	*Salt to taste*
two), cubed	*1 egg, beaten*

Melt the butter in the top of a double boiler. Add the cubed cheese and cook until just melted. Add beer slowly, then spices, and then the beaten egg a little at a time. Serve hot over whole wheat toast.

Serves two generously.

CELERY FLAKES Dehydrated celery leaves, called flakes, can be used in much the same manner as dried parsley, particularly in cream sauces and soups.

CELERY SALT The mineral content of celery is very high, and when the vegetable is dehydrated it produces a nutritious salty seasoning that tastes like—celery! Sprinkle on all foods that ask for this flavorful touch.

CELERY SEED This aromatic celery-tasting seed can be used to flavor soups and cream or cottage cheese. A tea made from the seeds (1 teaspoon to 1 cup boiling water) is said to be of therapeutic value in the treatment of rheumatism.

CEREAL Commercial American cereals are devitalized to the point of absurdity. The only nonabsurd aspect is that people actually consume them! *Always* use whole grain cereals—unpopped, unpuffed, unsugarcoated. They will give you your money's worth as well as your health's worth, for straight untreated grains are far cheaper pound for pound than their "enriched" processed counterparts.

Whole grain nonprecooked cereals do take longer to prepare; on early winter mornings this is not always desirable. Here are a few short cuts: Use the finer ground cereals (such as buckwheat grits instead of buckwheat groats, finely ground steel-cut oats instead of coarsely ground, cracked wheat instead of whole kernel wheat); what you lose in texture you will gain in cooking time. Or use the thermos jar method: Fill a wide-mouthed thermos with hot water; let it stand while cooking ½ cup whole grain in 2 cups boiling water for a couple of minutes; then pour the water out of the thermos and pour in the cereal and its cooking water. Add ½ cup raisins or currants if you like; close tightly and lay thermos on its side. Wake up to steaming hot cereal, ready to eat instantly with honey and cream.

Toasted granola-type whole grain cereals are now popular items on the health market. They can be delicious as an instant cereal or dry snack; however, if you have any digestive or intestinal problems, be sure to soak them for a while before eating. Bircher-muesli, the original "health" cereal, has the nutritional advantage of being made of uncooked grain. When using packaged muesli, again presoak, if necessary, to soften grain and rocklike raisins. But why not make your own granola and muesli?

GRANOLA

6 c. oat flakes	⅔ c. honey
1 c. sesame seeds,	Optional:
unhulled raw	½ c. shredded
1 c. wheat germ, raw	coconut
Pinch of sea salt	1 c. raw peanuts
⅓ c. pressed oil	1 c. raisins

Mix together all ingredients (except raisins) with a wooden spoon, and spread out on a baking sheet. Bake in a 300-degree oven, stirring every 10 minutes, until light brown—about 30–40 minutes. While the granola cools, add raisins if desired. Store in a well-sealed container. Granola keeps well without refrigeration—so this recipe makes a goodly amount. If it becomes a little soggy after a while, simply recrisp it in the oven.

MUESLI

1 c. oat flakes	1 apple, grated
1 c. milk	1 tbsp. raisins
1 tbsp. lemon juice	1 tbsp. chopped hazelnuts
3 tbsp. honey	

Soak oat flakes in milk for 30 minutes. Add lemon juice, honey, grated apple (skin and all if it is organic), raisins, and nuts. Mix well.   Serves three.
Note: Any cereal flakes can substitute for the oats in muesli and granola: wheat, rye, barley, rice, soya, etc.

CHAMOMILE An old favorite among herbs, chamomile was cherished by the ancient Egyptians who claimed that its aromatic tea was a mild—but not to be disparaged!—elixir of youth. A more concrete value of this wild flower lies in its sedative power; brew yourself a cup of chamomile tea (1 teaspoon chamomile to 1 cup boiling water and steep 10 minutes) before going to bed, add a little honey, and sleep will find you with utmost speed! Even the illustrious young Peter Rabbit was sent to bed with a calming cup of chamomile after his adventures in Farmer MacGregor's garden.

The tea is calming for nervous conditions in women; it regulates menstruation and alleviates cramps. It is soothing in instances of indigestion and neuralgia. Administer a mild dose of tea to infants for alleviation of teething pains. A compress soaked in a strong solution of chamomile tea will ease irritation of inflamed areas of skin—you might try this for complexion problems. If you want to make your blond hair blonder, by all means try a chamomile rinse. It's very simple: Boil ½ ounce chamomile flowers in a pint of water for 20 minutes; strain and pour over hair after washing.

CHARCOAL Charcoal has a remarkable ability to absorb fermenting gases and poisonous substances; it lends itself to many uses. Charcoal filters have been used for many years to draw out noxious substances from drinking water. Butter carefully packed in charcoal will keep for a year. A small bag of charcoal kept in the silverware drawer will absorb the sulphur gases that cause tarnish. In drawers, closets, and poorly ventilated rooms a bag of charcoal pieces will absorb musty odors.

Medicinally, charcoal will alleviate gaseous conditions, heartburn, and dysentery. If administered immediately following accidental poisoning, it will help to draw some of the poison away from the body. (In case of poisoning, however, your first step, of course, is to call a doctor!) A poultice made of powdered charcoal can alleviate skin conditions—burns, bruises, inflammation of the eyes. Charcoal comes in powder and pill form and should be made of the finest soft woods.

CHEESE All cheeses are made of coagulated milk, but the methods of aging cheese are so innumerable and the types of milk used so various, that we are faced in our lifetimes with the happy prospect of savoring hundreds upon hundreds of deliciously different kinds of cheese.

The character of a cheese depends on whether cow, goat, sheep, or buffalo milk is used; on how much cream is added to or left out of the milk; on what kind of coagulator is used (nowadays this is usually rennin, an enzyme taken from the stomach of a calf, but in times gone by vinegar, fig juice, decoctions of thistle tops and artichoke flowers were also used); on how long the cheese is aged (this can be anywhere from two days to two years). Spices, wines, or herbs may be added to lend distinctive flavor.

Cheese-making used to be a local farmhouse activity. Farmer Brown's cheese would be different from neighbor Jones' because their cows grazed on opposite sides of the dirt road. Today, however, cheese markets are monopolized and degraded by giant concerns. We find "Swiss" cheese made in Wisconsin and "Italian fontina" made in Sweden. Inevitably taste and quality suffer.

And then there are the additives (not to mention pesticide residues, an enormous problem)—stabilizers, emulsifiers, dyes, bleaches, preservatives. Ever wonder why cream cheese and cottage cheese will last for six weeks in your refrigerator? Try making your own (see recipes below) and you will find that if the delicious stuff is not eaten in three days or so it starts to ferment and then to mold—that is a healthy sign! Always rejoice if you find a forgotten piece of cheese that has gone moldy on you; that means it is alive. There are Wisconsin "Swiss" cheeses that can sit looking beautiful in the icebox for *months* with absolutely no change in appearance or flavor—just imagine the unwholesome chemicals that must be used to produce such an unnatural state of affairs.

Try to buy traditionally made regional cheeses. There are still true Vermont cheddars and smoked Oregon tillamooks and homemade Italian ricottas around. Try to find cheese made from the milk of organically raised cows, and if possible, from certified raw milk. Then you will enjoy the full benefits of the calcium and protein with which cheese abounds, without fear of pesticide contamination. *Never* resort to processed cheese.

It is prepared from ground-up low-quality cheese and made smooth or spreadable by the addition of harmful emulsifiers. There are still many good European cheeses available to us, but they too have their problems with pesticide residues and additives. Whether native or foreign, try to buy cheese that you can watch being cut from its original large piece; often additives are listed on a large round of cheese but omitted when it is repackaged in small pieces.

Here are some recipes for naturally curdled cheeses that can easily be made at home. They will show you what good fresh cheese should taste like.

CREAM CHEESE

Let a pint of heavy cream sour at room temperature. This will take about 2 days. Pour into a cheesecloth bag and let it drain. When solid, refrigerate.

COTTAGE CHEESE

Heat 2 quarts milk in a large enamel pot until barely lukewarm. Place covered in a warm spot—in the sun in summer, or in the stove in winter (warm the oven every once in a while to keep the temperature at about 85 degrees). In 1 or 2 days the curd will have risen to the top and the whey will be on the bottom. Put curd in a colander lined with a piece of cheesecloth, drain, then draw up cloth and squeeze out as much liquid as possible. Makes about 14 ounces of cheese.
This can be flavored with salt, caraway seeds, chopped chives, etc. If a harder cheese is desired, more like mozzarella, keep the milk at a slightly higher temperature—about 115 degrees.

These cheeses can be used to make:

COEUR A LA CREME

½ c. cottage cheese
½ c. cream cheese
½ c. heavy cream

¼ c. "raw" sugar
1 tbsp. kirsch (or ¼ tsp. vanilla)

37

Cream all together. Press into traditional heart-shaped baskets or porcelain molds, lined with cheesecloth. Chill for 2 hours. Unmold and serve with jam or fresh fruit.
Serves four.

CHERRY, DRIED The cherry is said to be effective in the treatment of gout and arthritis and as such has taken its stand on dried food shelves. It is high in vitamin C; syrup made from the dried or fresh fruit is a time-honored cough remedy.

CHERRY BARK TEA The dried inner bark of the North American wild cherry tree is used to make this tea. It is useful in the treatment of mucous coughs and asthma and is said to strengthen the stomach. To brew, steep 1 teaspoon bark in 1 cup of boiling water for 3 to 5 minutes.

CHERVIL A delicate herb for the educated palate, this fernlike leaf of the carrot family lends sweet fragrance to salads, cream soups, *sauce béarnaise*, and *aux fines herbes*. Planted in fall and harvested in spring, chervil has long been used as a spring tonic; it is said to have blood-cleansing and diuretic qualities. Use it generously in the kitchen—it never overpowers but rather enhances other herbal flavors.

CHESTNUT Chestnuts have graced the tables of Europe for centuries in the widest variety of forms, from the exalted *marron glacé* to the common porridge. The chestnut is rich in potassium, and contains good quantities of sodium and magnesium. It can be used as a potato substitute, for unlike other nuts, the chestnut is predominantly starchy rather than oily. Macrobiotics cherish it for its yang characteristics.

To prepare fresh chestnuts for cooking: With a sharp knife cut two slits in a cross form on the nut; bake in a hot oven until they split; peel (if your mouth is watering, stop here—they're delicious!). To prepare dried chestnuts for cooking: Soak overnight in water; if they are to be cooked in ample water an hour or more, presoaking is unnecessary.

CHESTNUT RICE

2½ c. water

1½ tsp. salt

1 c. brown rice

½ c. dried chestnuts

2 chopped scallions (or 1 medium onion)

2 tbsp. butter

Bring salted water to boil. Add rice so slowly that water does not stop boiling. Add dried chestnuts. Cover tightly and simmer about 45 minutes, or until water is absorbed and rice is fluffy. Meanwhile sauté chopped scallions in butter. When chestnut rice is ready, toss with scallion butter and serve.

Serves four.

CHIA SEED The minuscule black chia seeds are gathered from a type of wild sage that is found in the southwest United States and in Mexico. Their energizing value was well-known to the American Indians, who made use of the potent seeds to sustain them on long desert marches. Chia seeds have a very high protein content.

The seeds (which are virtually tasteless) are most commonly used sprinkled over a bowl of morning cereal—a tablespoon will

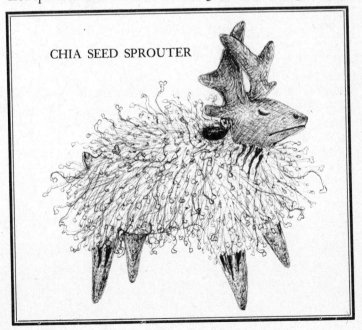

CHIA SEED SPROUTER

do. When using the whole seed, soak for a few hours before using; but chia seeds are extremely mucilaginous, and after a little soaking they become rather jellylike. We prefer to grind the seeds in a blender and then sprinkle the meal directly on the cereal. This meal can also be added to peanut butter, cottage cheese, bread dough—and just about anything else that hits your fancy.

Chia seeds cannot be sprouted in the conventional manner because of their highly mucilaginous nature. However, if you can put your hands on one of the hollow Mexican earthenware animals that are made especially for the purpose (see illustration), you will have a green blanket of protein-rich chia sprouts ready for the plucking.

CHICK-PEA   The curious name that English has fastened to this Asiatic legume is merely a phonetic adaptation of the original Latin *Cicer* and the French *pois chiche*—there is truly nothing to do with young chickens here! Chick-peas grow one or two to the pod and are a valuable food, rich in calcium, potassium, sodium, iron, phosphorus, and protein. They are available to us only in dry form and must be soaked in water overnight and then simmered for 3 hours (or until tender) before serving.

Chick-peas and rice with a little rosemary, butter, salt, and pepper make a delicious dish; add some chicken broth and you will have transformed this into a tasty soup. Cooled and seasoned with salad dressing, chick-peas make a refreshing summer salad or all-season antipasto. Here follows a zestful dip for bread or crackers—though you may end eating it by the spoonful—a version of the Middle Eastern *hummus*.

CHICK-PEA PUREE (HUMMUS)

2 c. chick-peas, soaked and cooked (see above)

½ c. olive or sesame seed oil (preferably pressed oil)

⅓ c. fresh lemon juice

3 cloves garlic, finely chopped

½ tsp. salt

½ c. sesame tahini (crushed sesame seed paste, optional)

CHICK-PEA
Plant– ½ size
Seeds–life-size

To prepare in blender: Put all ingredients in a blender except chick-peas; blend well. Slowly add chick-peas; blend to a smooth paste. If too thick, add a little water. If you have no blender, mash the chick-peas thoroughly and mix in the other ingredients well. Serve cold.

CHICORY   Where would the coffee of France and New Orleans be without its chicory? For it is the mixture of the roasted chicory root with the coffee bean that yields the distinctive brew of these areas. (Purist coffee lovers might call this adulteration rather than mixture.)

Chicory is a wild plant that is often brought under cultivation (more in Europe than in the United States); its delicate blue flowers open and then close again with clocklike regularity in the morning hours. The plant shares many of the medicinal and culinary uses of its relative the dandelion. Its tasty bitter leaves act as a stimulant to the appetite and digestion and can be eaten raw in salad or cooked as a vegetable. The leaves can also be chopped and brewed as a tea that is useful for liver ailments, gout, and rheumatism. The chicory root, ground and roasted, is used as a coffee substitute, and when combined with coffee is said to counteract its stimulating effects.

CHIVES   This most refined member of the onion family is mild in taste, has a stimulating effect on the appetite, and has none of the digestion-disturbing tendencies of the onion. The leaves are the most used part of the plant (when growing your own, do not encourage the beautiful blue flowers; they toughen the herb, although the tiny bulbs can be pickled as an unusual delicacy). Frozen chives should be reconstituted in a little water before using. Add this chopped greenery to vichyssoise, salads, and omelets; simultaneously you will be adding good supplies of vitamins A and C and of potassium to your diet.

CINNAMON   True cinnamon is cultivated in much of the tropical world, including South America, the Pacific, Africa, and tropical Asia. The bark is cut off the cinnamon tree in long strips and slowly dried into "quills"—those long curling tubular cinnamon sticks with which we are familiar. Often used to adulterate ground cinnamon is "cassia," or Chinese cinnamon, which is more easily and widely cultivated (and therefore cheaper) and has a taste very similar to real cinnamon, though more pungent and less delicate. So if you want to be sure of your cinnamon, buy it in stick form.

Cinnamon was highly prized in ancient times as a perfume, medicine, preservative, and flavoring spice; small quantities of the precious quills were considered fit gifts for kings. The Arabs, who first brought cinnamon to the West, shrouded its origins in grotesque mysteries to frighten off rival traders. As you stir your espresso with a cinnamon quill and nibble on a cinnamon cookie, imagine yourself the envy of ancient potentates and bedaggered Arabs.

CARROT CAKE

2 c. whole wheat pastry flour
2 tsp. baking soda
1 tsp. salt
2 tsp. cinnamon

¼ c. vegetable oil (preferably pressed oil)
1½ c. honey
4 eggs, well beaten
3½ c. grated carrots

Sift together the flour, soda, salt, and cinnamon. Stir in oil and honey, and then the well-beaten eggs. Mix in the grated carrots. Oil and flour two 8-inch layer pans or one 8-inch spring pan. Pour in batter and bake in a 350-degree oven for 35 minutes. Remove from pans and cool on a cake rack while you prepare the cream cheese frosting below—also delicious unfrosted.

CREAM CHEESE FROSTING

8 oz. cream cheese
¼ lb. butter

3 c. powdered sugar (preferably "raw" sugar powdered in blender)

Have cream cheese and butter at room temperature. Cream together, using a spoon or fingers. Add powdered sugar until desired consistency is reached. Makes enough frosting for a two-layer cake.

CLEANSING AGENTS, BIODEGRADABLE

A number of cleansing agents that claim to be the answer to detergent pollution are sold in health food stores. They are said to be soap-free and detergent-free, nonirritating to the skin, biodegradable, and the answer to every cleaning problem from hair and dishes to cars and floors. The formulas of these cleansers are of course trade secrets, so one must accept on faith (or not accept!) their claims of organicness and biodegradability. Certain brands do have the advantage of being easy on the skin—both infant and adult—of making gentle playful bubbles in the children's bath, of making old clothes seem brighter in color, of working well in both hot and cold water, and of producing foam that disappears quickly down a small drain without all the usual painful coaxing.

CLOVE   The dried flower buds of the large evergreen clove tree form this nail-shaped spice. The name "clove" is derived from the French *clou*, meaning nail. Originally native to the Molucca (or Spice) Islands, the clove tree was smuggled out to other islands with intricate subterfuge by spice-hungry colonialist nations.

The clove is now used primarily as a culinary spice, and its oil for the alleviation of toothache. But its uses are far more varied. To chew a clove sweetens the breath, and ancient Chinese officials were once allowed to approach their monarch only when holding cloves in their mouths. A few cloves brewed with Oriental tea add enticing flavor, as well as giving a carminative effect to the tea. In a container of water set on a radiator, they will deodorize a room. Mulled wine flavored with cloves offers a more exciting way to aid the digestion than most commercial concoctions.

In the kitchen, use cloves sparingly, for their flavor is heavy. Try tossing an onion studded with a few cloves into your next pot of stew or rice.

On rainy autumn days your children might enjoy the sweet-smelling activity of pomander-ball making; they will be ready in time for Christmas giving.

44

POMANDER BALLS

Oranges, thin-skinned   *Cinnamon, powdered*
Cloves aplenty

Make sure the oranges are a thin-skinned variety, or there will be sore fingers at the end of this game. For added protection, Band-Aids can be placed for padding on appropriate fingers—what child will not love an excuse for a Band-Aid! Stud each orange all over with cloves, pushing them right in to their tops. Roll studded oranges in powdered cinnamon, and pat on a heavy coating. Wrap each fruit in tissue paper and cure it for about six weeks. Then shake off excess cinnamon and the pomanders are ready to impart their sweet smell to closets and cupboards.

COCONUT, SHREDDED   The tall slender coconut tree lends itself to myriad uses. Its trunk is used for timber, its flower spathes for crude sugar and toddy and arrack liquor, its leaves for basket-weaving and roofing, its husk for rope-making, its shells for drinking vessels, and its kernels for oil and coconut milk and "meat." Coconut palms are found growing in tropical countries throughout the world, particularly on seacoasts, for the rounded triangular-shaped coconut is easily carried by ocean currents to far-off shores.

Shredded coconut is made from the meat of the coconut, the white inner lining of the kernel. It is used primarily in the preparation of desserts, for its sweet nutty flavor. Commercially you will find it in both moist and dry form; moist coconut has more unpleasant additives than the dry, but both are likely to be sweetened with unhealthful sugar—which is foolishness, for coconut is loaded with its own valuable natural sugar. So buy it dessicated and without additives at your health food store. Or if you are handy with a knife and steady of arm, prepare your own, it will be naturally moist, utterly delicious, and very economical.

Coconut meat will add protein, potassium, phosphorus, magnesium, and a touch of iodine to your desserts. It is low in carbohydrates and contains less fat than most other nuts.

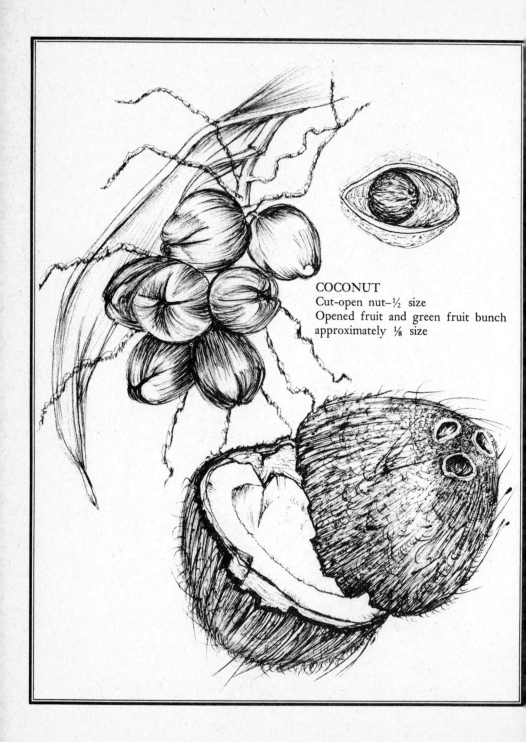

COCONUT
Cut-open nut–½ size
Opened fruit and green fruit bunch
approximately ⅛ size

FRESH SHREDDED COCONUT

If you can hear the milk lapping inside the coconut when you shake it, it is ripe and ready. Pierce the "eyes" of the coconut with a screwdriver and drain out the milk (you can drink this on the spot, or use it as liquid in any dessert recipe—it is very nutritious).

Put coconut in a 400-degree oven for 15–20 minutes. Remove it from the oven and immediately give coconut a sharp blow with a hammer, and the shell will fall away from the meat. Trim off the dark skin. Grind the white meat in a blender. Keep it moist in a jar in the refrigerator; it will stay fresh for about two weeks. Or dry it slowly in the oven and it will not have to be refrigerated.

COCONUT UPSIDE DOWN CAKE

In a flat-bottomed 8-inch iron skillet melt:

6 tbsp. butter	*Add: 1½ c. fresh*
½ c. "raw" or brown	*shredded coconut (or*
sugar	*dessicated coconut*
	plus 2 tbsp. water)

BATTER

1½ c. whole wheat	*1 egg plus 1 egg yolk,*
pastry flour	*well beaten*
2½ tsp. baking powder	*½ tsp. vanilla extract*
½ tsp. salt	*½ c. coconut (or dairy)*
½ c. butter	*milk*
¾ cup sugar (preferably	
"raw" sugar)	

Sift flour, baking powder, and salt three times. Cream butter, sugar, eggs, and vanilla. Mix half of creamed mixture into dry ingredients, then half of the liquid, then the other half of creamed mixture, then the last half of liquid. Do not overmix. Pour into skillet on top of coconut. Bake at 350 degrees about 35 minutes. Remove from the oven, loosen the sides with a knife; immediately flip over onto a cake platter. Serve warm or cool.

COCONUT OIL Coconut oil, extracted from the copra or dried meat of the coconut kernel, is one of the most highly saturated of all vegetable oils. Note that many of the so-called "high in unsaturates" margarines use coconut oil as a hardening agent—an oil that is more saturated than butter itself!

Although coconut oil can be used for cooking purposes, it is most widely used in the manufacture of cosmetics. It is also said to be useful in mitigating muscular aches when massaged into the affected area, and in preventing stretch marks during pregnancy.

COFFEE SUBSTITUTES There was an anticoffee bandwagon long before health foodists appeared on the scene. When early Muslims began using coffee as a "devotional anti-soporific" to see them through lengthy religious services, they stirred up fierce controversy with orthodox priests who regarded coffee as a forbidden intoxicant. Later, in the sixteenth century, the establishment of coffeehouses in Constantinople excited the wrath of the ecclesiastics, for they cut down on church attendance. In England the first coffeehouses were established in the seventeenth century and aroused the hostility of King Charles II himself, who claimed that they were a "disturbance to the peace and quiet of the nation" and harbored undesirable dissidents.

These rocky times passed, however. The raising of coffee became an enormously lucrative enterprise and spread from its native Abyssinia to all tropical parts of the world. The roasted seeds of the red fruit of the coffee plant began to be held in high regard as an alleviator of fatigue and sustainer of strength under stress.

Not until the twentieth century has coffee been strongly attacked on purely dietary grounds. Now we hear that it raises the blood sugar level of the body at an alarming rate, that it aggravates ulcers and heart conditions, that it leads to vitamin B deficiency, that it is habit-forming, that mixed with cream it is bad for the digestion, that it is full of harmful caffeine and tannic acid . . . And so, we have the coffee substitutes: roasted grains, figs, beans, dandelion roots, chicory roots. No one will argue that the substitutes are indeed more healthful than coffee, and there are those who may find them toothsome. The only trouble is, they just don't taste much like coffee.

If you persist in sticking with the real thing, you can palliate the bad effects somewhat by brewing coffee with the filter or espresso methods, which are said to release less tannic acid into your cup. Also a snack of sunflower seeds (or other protein food) may help to prolong the "high" you get from your cup of coffee, by shoring it up with a real energy source.

COLTSFOOT TEA The yellow-flowered coltsfoot (*Tussilago farfara*), whose leaves are shaped like the hoof of a colt, may be found growing in moist soils and alongside streams in Europe, Canada, and northeastern United States. It is most conspicuous in early spring, when its dandelionlike flowers appear. Although all parts of the plant possess some medicinal qualities, it is the fragrant leaves that are used for teas and poultices. As a tea high in vitamin C, coltsfoot is used to allay coughing; as an expectorant it helps to clean the respiratory tract. A cloth moistened in coltsfoot tea and applied to the throat or chest will relieve those areas of congestion. To prepare coltsfoot tea, steep 1 teaspoon leaves in 1 cup boiling water for 30 minutes.

COMFREY TEA Knitbone, boneset, healing herb—these popular names for comfrey are indicative of its extraordinary medicinal qualities. It is particularly well known for its ability to speed the healing of fractured and broken bones; either the roots or the leaves are pounded into a mucilaginous mass and applied as a poultice to the injured area, and in addition the tea is taken internally. Comfrey poultices have been said to effect wondrous cures of malignant ulcers; again tea from either root or leaf is taken conjointly, internally. Comfrey tea is also useful in the treatment of chest disorders and tuberculosis, internal ulcers, and diarrhea. To prepare the tea, steep 1 teaspoon leaves or root in 1 cup boiling water for 30 minutes.

Comfrey (*Symphytum officinale*) grows wild in many parts of the world, including North America. It is also easily cultivated as a garden plant and can be cooked and eaten like spinach.

CORIANDER The name of this aromatic spice gives no indication of its culinary potential—"coriander" is derived from the Greek *coris*, an ill-smelling bug whose odor was thought to be similar to that of fresh coriander seed. Only when dried, does the seed assume the goodly character that lends itself so well to dessert-making, curries, and many South American dishes. Tea made from the crushed seeds is carminative; the flavorful seeds can also be mixed with herbs and spices whose taste alone might be unpalatable.

Coriander leaves, which look rather like those of the carrot, add unusual seasoning to salads and soups—no problem with odors here, for the leaves are delicious fresh or dried.

CORN, FLAKED Do not confuse this with the corn-flake of supermarket breakfast cereal notoriety. This is the crushed whole kernel of corn, with all its natural goodness intact. Unlike most whole flaked grains, which have only to be soaked before eating, these corn flakes require light cooking. See also *Cornmeal*.

CORN FLOUR Finely ground kernels of corn yield a flour—white, yellow, or (in the Southwest) blue, depending on the type of corn used—that has a distinctive corn taste, but does not have the mealy texture one usually associates with ground corn products. It is good added to soups and stews as a thickener and can be substituted in bread recipes for a portion of wheat flour. If you feel adventurous, try using it instead of meal in cornmeal recipes—you will be inventing a new dish all your own, and one bound to taste good. See also *Cornmeal*.

CORN GRITS Coarser in grind than cornmeal, but finer of course than flaked corn, these grits make a grand breakfast cereal. They are far more nutritious than the traditional white hominy grits, which are dehulled and degermed. Corn grits can also be used for making a more textured polenta or cornmeal mush. See also *Cornmeal*.

CORN KERNEL, DRIED Dried corn kernels are for those who prefer to grind their own meal. . . . And that cannot be beat! These kernels are not meant for cooking; they take forever and a day to soften. See also *Cornmeal*.

CORN OIL   One of the most unsaturated of vegetable oils, this oil is ideal for all types of cooking and can also be used for salad dressings. Be sure to buy it in as unprocessed a state as possible. Aim for crude pressed corn oil, though it is hard to find. A darker color will be one indication that the oil contains more of its natural qualities.

CORN-SILK TEA   Fresh or dried corn silk, steeped 1 teaspoon to a cup of boiling water, is said to be beneficial for kidney and bladder ailments.

CORNMEAL   Controversy has long waged over the origins of the genus *Zea mays*, or maize—or if you will, common corn. There are those who assert that it is strictly American in origin; certainly the American Indians were master corn cultivators long before Europeans set foot on these shores. Others claim that corn reached Europe from the East with the Arab invasions into Spain in the thirteenth century. In Italy, where cornmeal cookery has attained a fine art, the name for corn is *granturco*—Turkish grain—which certainly points to an eastern origin.

Well, East or West, it is a superb food! Nutritionally it contains less protein and niacin than other grains, but unless your diet consists of absolutely nothing but refined cornmeal, your chances of getting pellagra—that old bugbear of cornmeal—are entirely nil. White cornmeal is milled from white corn and is said by some connoisseurs to have a more sophisticated flavor and smooth texture than meal from yellow corn. Yellow cornmeal, on the other hand, has a fuller taste and is more nutritious, for it contains carotene, which is converted by the body into vitamin A.

Never buy degerminated, overmilled, overheated, synthetic-vitamin-enriched commercial cornmeal—it has little health value and even less taste. Among properly milled whole kernel meals, flavor will vary depending on the type of corn used; buy in small quantities until you find the taste that pleases you. Tex-

51

ture is also a variant; some distributors label as "meal" grinds that are more like flour in fineness. What joy to be able to choose and not be constricted to standardized lifeless products!

COSMETICS The field of cosmetics is difficult to deal with, for on the plea of guarding secret formulas, cosmetic firms are not required to state the contents of their wares. Ordinary cosmetics, of even the best-known brands, have often been found to produce highly allergenic and injurious reactions. The idea behind "organic" cosmetics is certainly a valid one, that the ingredients be derived from natural food and herb substances, with all their inherent vitamins, minerals, and proteins. But which "organic" products are truly organic remains a matter for investigation—and your own experimentation.

While you are shopping around for the perfect solution to your skin and hair needs, make do with these safe and sure (and inexpensive) home treatments:

FOR THE FACE

Dry skin—spread beaten egg yolk on skin; wash off after 10 minutes.
Medium skin—use good-quality mayonnaise in the same manner.
Oily skin—use beaten egg white as above; but not too often, as this is very astringent.

FOR DRY SKIN

Spread pressed vegetable oil instead of lotion on dry areas of the body; you will be surprised at how quickly it is absorbed.

FOR THE HAIR

Three suggestions for soft, shiny, manageable hair:
Before washing, massage vegetable oil or mayonnaise into scalp and hair; leave it there for 20 minutes; then wash hair as usual. Be prepared, however, to give it the necessary time: It takes a lot of washing to get that healthful oil or mayonnaise out!
After washing, rub a beaten egg into hair and scalp.

This rinses out easily.

Or use one part apple cider vinegar to three parts water as a rinse after washing. You might keep a jar of this simple solution in the bathroom and splash it all over the body after bathing. It will tighten the pores and is very refreshing.

COTTONSEED FLOUR The flour made from ground cottonseed is packed with nutritious components; it is extremely high in protein, calcium, and phosphorus and contains good quantities of iron, thiamine, riboflavin, and niacin. Only trouble is, there is no such thing as organically raised cotton, and therefore all products deriving from it are subject to pesticide contamination. Another problem is gossypol, a toxic natural pigment that occurs in cottonseed. The amount retained when meal is made of the seeds varies with the species and the process, but it is almost always present. Some health food stores refuse to sell the product on these grounds; others feel that the outstanding nutritional value outweighs the dangers. Take your choice.

This flour can be used as a substitute for about 7 percent of other flour in any recipe, to increase vitamin, mineral, and protein content.

COTTONSEED OIL Cottonseed oil is a very good source of linoleic oil, an essential fatty acid that is absolutely necessary in everyone's diet. It ranks with corn and soybean oil as one of the principal sources of this important ingredient. However, it is probably impossible to find cottonseed oil that is not contaminated by insecticide spray. See also *Cottonseed Flour*.

COUSCOUS The basic dish of North African cuisine, couscous can be extremely intricate to prepare, or utterly simple, depending on your approach. This is a semolina made from hard durum wheat—rich in gluten and protein—coarsely ground, but finer than either bulgur or cracked wheat. The traditional manner of preparing couscous calls for a *cous-*

cousière, a colander tightly fitted over a base pot; a meat stew is placed in the bottom, and the couscous in the colander top to cook in the steam of the stew.

Here is a simple dish that can be made with ordinary Western kitchen utensils. Perhaps it will inspire you to delve into the more complex aspects of traditional couscous preparation.

COUSCOUS WITH SHRIMP

1 c. couscous	*5 tbsp. butter*
2 tbsp. butter	*6 tbsp. soy sauce*
2 c. boiling water	*1 tsp. powdered ginger*
1 lb. shrimp, shelled and deveined	

Sauté couscous in 2 tablespoons butter for 1 minute; then add boiling water and simmer, while stirring, for about 3 minutes. Cover, and let sit for 15 minutes while you cook the shrimp.
Sauté the shrimp in 5 tablespoons butter, soy sauce, and powdered ginger for 5 to 8 minutes, depending on size of shrimp. When shrimp is cooked (firm but tender), stir in the couscous. Serve with a large fresh salad.

A quick and delicious dinner for four.

CRACKED WHEAT   See *Wheat, Cracked*.

CUMIN   Feeling squeamish? Take cumin with your bread or wine, prescribes Pliny. Cumin is also supposed to induce a pallid complexion, and Pliny tells of students who took cumin to achieve that "studious" look. This herbaceous annual is native to Egypt, but long ago spread to Mediterranean shores, and is now cultivated worldwide. Cumin resembles caraway in appearance and taste—but it is more bitter. Widely used in Mexican chili powders and Indian curries, it can also be added to breads, cookies, rice, and creamed dishes for an interesting variation on the more familiar caraway flavor.

CURRANT, DRIED   Currants grow on shrublike plants that flourish both in the wild and under cultivation. They are akin to gooseberries, and the small rather translucent berries can be of black, red, or white variety. When fresh, they are used for pies, jellies, and wines. The black currant is the most commonly cultivated, dried, and sold commercially.

Dried black currants are rich in iron and vitamin C, are neat to eat, and delicious too. An interesting alternative to raisins, they are not as strong tasting. Substitute them in any recipe that calls for raisins; their smallness does not interfere with the slicing of bread and cutting of cookies the way large raisins sometimes tend to do. The delicate flavor of currants lends itself to exotic recipes, such as spiced rice or stuffed mussels and grape leaves.

RICE WITH CURRANTS AND NUTS

3 c. water (or broth)
1 tsp. salt
1½ c. brown rice
3 tbsp. pignoli nuts
⅓ c. dried currants

2 tbsp. butter
¾ tsp. allspice, powdered
¼ tsp. cinnamon,
  powdered

Bring salted water to boil; sprinkle in rice without stopping boiling. Cover and simmer. Gently sauté nuts and currants in the butter. After rice has cooked about 30 minutes, add sautéed nuts and currants with butter, allspice, and cinnamon. Continue cooking for about 15 minutes or until rice is tender and fluffy.

Serves four.

CURRY POWDER This Indian condiment is composed of a large and variable number of herbs and spices. A conservative tally of basic ingredients yields: red and black pepper, cardamom, cinnamon, coriander, cumin, fenugreek, garlic, ginger, mustard, turmeric, poppy seed. Each brand of curry powder uses its own variation of the basic recipe, and the results in your cooking pot will range from fiery hot to merely spicy. Diehard curry enthusiasts grind their own powder from freshly obtained ingredients.

The flavor of curry blends well with any number of foods and need not be limited to traditional main dishes. A dash in your salad dressing, creamed soups, egg dishes, and melted butter for vegetables will add new life to a meal.

CURRIED CHICKEN BREASTS

4 pair of chicken breasts,
* skinned and boned*
Juice of 2 lemons
⅔ c. whole wheat flour

¼ tsp. salt
2 tsp. butter
2 tsp. vegetable oil (pref-
* erably pressed oil)*

SAUCE

2 tbsp. butter
¾ c. finely chopped
* onion*
1 clove garlic, finely
* chopped*
1 small cooking apple,
* cored and chopped*
* (peel only if not*
* organically grown)*

3 tbsp. curry powder
2 tbsp. whole wheat flour
2 c. chicken broth
½ c. cream or yogurt
1 tsp. lemon juice
1 tbsp. grated lemon rind
* (preferably from un-*
* dyed organic lemon)*
Pinch of cayenne pepper

If you bone your own chicken breasts (not difficult), use the bones to make the 2 cups of broth for sauce, by simmering them for 3 hours in salted water.

Cut boned and skinned chicken into small pieces, about 8 to each breast. Dip each piece in lemon juice, then in mixture of flour and salt. Brown in butter and oil. Set aside in warm casserole.

In same pan, add butter and sauté onion and garlic until transparent. Add apple and cook slowly until soft. Add curry powder and flour and make a smooth paste, adding broth a little at a time, and then the cream. Bring sauce to boil, stirring the while, then cook partially covered over very low heat for about 20 minutes. Add lemon juice and rind. Taste to see if sauce is hot enough; if not, add a little cayenne pepper, but be careful not to overdo it—the taste of cayenne increases with cooking.

Pour sauce over chicken and stir to coat all pieces. Cook over low heat for half an hour. Serve immediately or set aside for later serving—even the next day.

Serve on a large bed of brown rice and with bowls of any of the following condiments:

chutney	*shredded unsweetened*
chopped scallions	*coconut*
diced avocado	*chopped salted peanuts*
diced pineapple	*or almonds*
dried currants marinated	*crumbled hard-boiled*
in brandy	*eggs*
	roasted pignoli nuts

Serves four royally.

 DAIKON, DRIED Daikon is a large white Japanese radish with a yin or acid tendency. When dried, it is long and stringlike and should be soaked for several hours before using. Chop it, sauté it, add salt and tamari sauce; also good with rice or other sautéed vegetables.

DANDELION If you are accustomed to viewing the common dandelion as a garden nuisance—stop! This vitamin-and-mineral-packed herb can be of great value to your health. Pick the plant in spring, when its leaves are young and tender; slice and cook the roots as a delicate vegetable, and use the leaves raw in salads for a zesty dish loaded with vitamin A. Persons on salt-restricted diets should go easy on the dandelions, however, for they contain large amounts of sodium. The yellow blossoms (if there are any left after your spring pickings) are traditionally used to make dandelion wine—a great favorite during Prohibition years in the United States.

You are most likely to find dandelion on the store shelf in the form of tea or as a coffee substitute. The tea, made from dried dandelion leaves, is considered an excellent blood cleanser, and is helpful to digestion, liver, and gallbladder. Its chopped roasted roots are used as a coffee substitute, which unfortunately does not taste a great deal like coffee but possesses the same curative values as the tea.

DATE, DRIED The tall and stately date palm has been cultivated in North Africa, the Middle East, and India since remote antiquity, and the date and its by-products have long been dietary staples in these areas. There the date is eaten fresh —an end-all of epicurean delights—or pounded into cakes, or ground to a flour, or its sap is rendered to sugar or made into various fermented beverages. The Spaniards in the eighteenth century introduced the date palm into California, where it now thrives.

The date is rich in minerals such as potassium, magnesium, iron, and phosphorus, and in various B vitamins. It also has a very high sugar content. Dried dates make an extremely nutritious snack for children and are a great help in unseating the ubiquitous candy bar. They have a constipating tendency, the opposite of most other dried fruits. During the drying process, they are often treated with sulphuric acid; make sure to buy organically grown unsulphured dates.

For a special treat, try stuffing dates with nut butter or nut meats—peanut butter and pecans go particularly well with dates.

DATE-NUT TARTS

Pastry for a double-crust
    pie
2 eggs, beaten
½ c. honey
¼ tsp. salt

½ c. finely chopped
    dates
½ c. chopped pecans or
    walnuts
1 tsp. vanilla
¼ c. melted butter

Roll out dough on floured board and cut into rounds (a 4-inch diameter piece of pastry will fit into a muffin form of 1¾-inch diameter). Press into muffin tins. Makes about one dozen.
Beat eggs well. Add honey and salt and beat vigorously. Stir in dates, nuts, vanilla, and butter. Fill each pastry cup about ¾ full with this mixture. Bake 25 minutes at 350 degrees or until browned and center is firm.

DATE SUGAR   Date sugar can be made from the sap of the date palm. The date sugar that is most commonly seen in this country, however, is composed of ground dried dates. As dates have a sugar content of about 70 percent, these rich brown granules offer an excellent mineral-rich substitute for honey or cane sugar. See also *Date, Dried*.

DATE SYRUP Date syrup is made of pulverized fresh dates. It makes a delicious and healthful sweet topping for yogurt, pancakes, waffles, and desserts. It can also be used in baking to replace sugar, honey, or molasses.

DILL Don't imprison this delightful herb in the pickle jar! Its uses as a tasty aromatic and a medicinal of long standing are far too various to accept such limitation. For hundreds of years dill tea has been used as a gentle sedative and as an aid to digestion. These attributes lend it power to calm nerves, hasten sleep, prevent nausea, increase the flow of a mother's milk, stop an infant's colic, even to chase away the hiccups. To make dill tea, steep ½ teaspoonful dill seed in a cup of hot water for 10 minutes; when administering to a baby, you can substitute milk for water.

In cooking, dill is just as useful. Dill salt, made from ground dill seeds, is a tasty salt substitute. Use either the seeds or the fresh or dried leaves sprinkled over salads, in cooking cabbage, in fish sauces (try dill with drawn butter) and broth, or mixed with cream cheese as a sandwich spread. Cucumbers and dill are a natural twosome; try serving this cucumber-yogurt soup with dill for a summer lunch with some good homemade bread beneath the cool shadows of a comfortable tree.

CUCUMBER-YOGURT SOUP WITH DILL

2 cucumbers	2 tbsp. chopped fresh dill
1 pt. yogurt	(or 1 tsp. ground dill
Salt and pepper to taste	weed)
Dash of Worchestershire	¼ tsp. cumin, ground
sauce	

Peel and finely chop cucumbers, or put through a blender. Put into soup tureen and add other ingredients. Mix well. Serve very cold with some extra dill sprinkled on top.

DULSE Extremely healthful and rich in organic iodine, fresh dulse, a dark red seaweed, is delicious in salads. Children in the maritime provinces of Canada chew on fresh dulse instead of candy. In health food stores dulse is found dried, and in this form it is quite leathery and tough; therefore it is usually used in cooking. Add it chopped to your soups, and forget the salt—dulse brings its own, in the most natural form possible.

DURUM WHEAT FLOUR This is a hard high-protein, high-gluten flour that is used for the making of pasta, semolina, and couscous. The grain is grown primarily in Russia, the United States, and Northern Africa.

EGGS, ORGANIC A good egg is hard to find! Today most hens live in overcrowded, disease-ridden, factory-type conditions—where a flock of 15,000 is considered small—without fresh air, natural light, or fresh food. They are fed antibiotics, methedrine, tranquilizers, chemicals to make the yolk appear more yellow, and additives to make the shell harder.

How does one find eggs from chickens whose feet still touch the old-fashioned earth? * If you live in the city it is a problem, and while a health food store can often provide you with a tasty (if expensive) solution, just as frequently it cannot. For in some large cities "organic" egg production has become industrialized; the result is eggs carefully classified as "fertile" and "nonfertile" and just as tasteless as the supermarket special—but far more costly. Try to find a store that deals with a specific farmer; or better still, take a drive and find the farmer yourself. It is worth the effort.

A healthy egg not only tastes better but is rich in protein, vitamins A, B, and D, and contains sodium, phosphorus, potassium, and lecithin—without contamination by cancerous cells and noxious chemicals. Fertile eggs are better for you than nonfertile eggs; but in mechanized egg production the rooster is just a nuisance—he eats too much and causes too much excite-

---

* Free-running chickens are also a tremendous natural control for insects—one of the factors which makes their eggs and meat that much richer than the ersatz products of the egg-chicken factories of today.

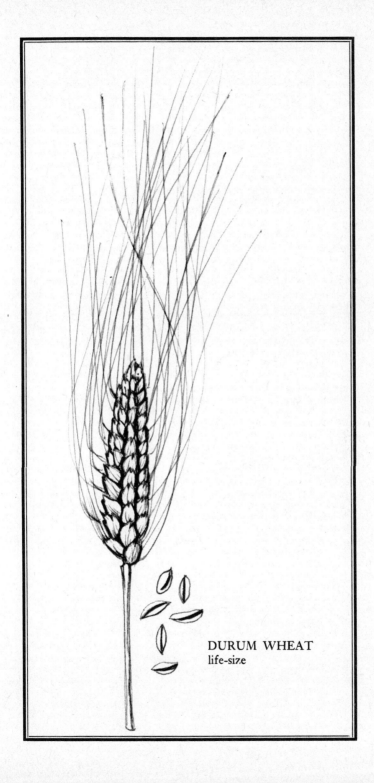

DURUM WHEAT
life-size

ment among the lucky hens. And fertile eggs cannot be made to last for weeks and weeks the way nonfertile ones can—all in all a poor risk in our money-conscious society. If your child is allergic to nonfertile eggs, try searching out some fertile ones for him; often those who are allergic to the one can tolerate the other very easily.

Tell how fresh an egg is by putting it in a bowl of water. If it sinks, it is fresh. If it floats, it is rotten. If it wavers in the middle, it is okay; don't try to poach it, and eat it in a hurry!

ELDERBERRY TEA Although elderberry tea is the most generally used, the common elder (*Sambucus canadensis* and *S. nigra*) also offers up as tea its bark, roots, leaves, and flowers, all of which have curative powers. Indeed, so many different remedies have been ascribed to the elder that in England, for example, it was called "the medicine chest of the country people." An infusion of the bruised leaves is said to repel mosquitoes, gnats, and even mice. A brew made from the bark is a purgative and emetic. The berries, however, yield the most pleasing tea. They are high in vitamin C and can be used for the treatment of colds and influenza. They increase perspiration, are diuretic, and are therefore useful as a blood cleanser. Cooled elderberry tea is very soothing when applied to the eyes.

The elder tree itself is steeped in legend. Old homes in England often have an elder planted nearby, for it was supposed to protect the inhabitants from witches. Judas is said to have hanged himself from an elder—the elder grows larger in Europe and the Middle East than in America—and the wood of the tree (there are several other sylvan candidates for the role) is reputed to have been used for the cross of Christ. Think on these things as you sip your cup of elderberry late at night by the fire.

EUCALYPTUS TEA The statuesque and aromatic eucalyptus tree, which sometimes reaches heights of 375 feet, is native to Australia and Tasmania. Now grown in many parts of the world, it is valued for its usefulness in reclaiming malarial areas and lands that are plagued by drought. And of course the eucalyptus has long had the distinction of its leaves being the sole diet of those wonderful koala bears. Though the long ovate leaves are reported to contain high amounts of hydrogen cyanide, their oil has long been recognized for its antiseptic qualities. The oil or crushed leaves can be applied to any surface skin wound with good results.

Tea made from the crushed leaves has an unusual bitter taste; it is said to be good for the digestion and useful for bronchial disorders. The vapors of the tea can also be inhaled in cases of asthma and chest congestion—the leaves used to be made into cigarettes which were smoked for these same illnesses.

 FAVA BEAN Fava (or broad) beans have been cultivated in Europe since the Iron Age; they are now also grown in the United States. These large lima-shaped beans are usually sold dried and are a very rich source of vitamin B, protein, phosphorus, iron, and calcium. Excellent additions to soup, they can also be served alone—cooked with a zestful sauce, for they tend to be bland in flavor.

Centuries ago Greeks and Romans believed that overindulgence in fava beans would impair the vision. Today among Mediterranean peoples (the most avid consumers of fava beans) there is a blood disorder known as favism, which is thought to be due to an overabundance of these beans in the diet. Such dire thoughts should not, however, interfere with enjoyment in moderation of this healthful and pleasant legume!

FAVA BEAN CASSEROLE

2 c. fava beans, dried
1 tsp. salt
4 medium-size onions,
    sliced
¼ c. butter
½ tsp. rosemary, dried
    crushed (or 1 tsp.
    fresh chopped)

½ tsp. salt
⅛ tsp. black pepper,
    freshly ground
6 fresh tomatoes, peeled,
    seeded, and chopped
    (or 3 c. canned
    tomatoes with juice,
    chopped)

Soak beans overnight in water to cover. Put them in a pot with the salt and soaking water, add more water if necessary, and simmer covered for 2 hours or until tender. Meanwhile sauté the sliced onions in butter; add rosemary, salt, and pepper. When the fava beans are

63

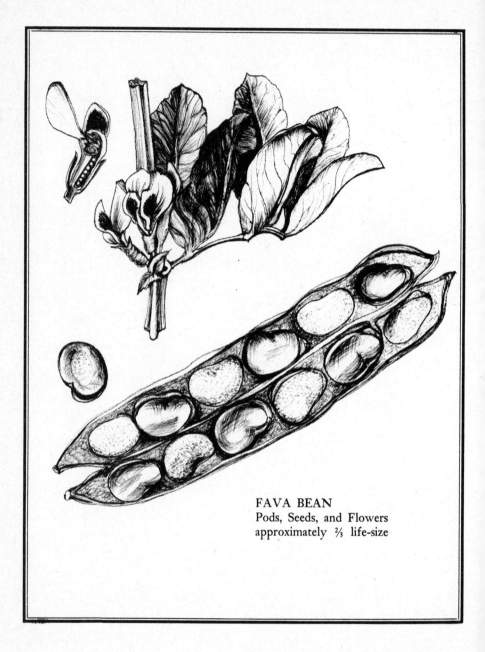

FAVA BEAN
Pods, Seeds, and Flowers
approximately ⅔ life-size

tender, mix them together with the onion mixture and the tomatoes. Turn into a casserole; cover and bake at 350 degrees for 1 hour. This hearty dish serves six as a side vegetable and four as a main course.

FENNEL Fennel can be found growing in almost every temperate climate; in California it grows wild in great profusion. Its uses are very similar to that of dill: The leaves are added to soups, salads, and fish. Toss a few fennel seeds in your next pot of baked beans—they will cut down on the gaseous effects of that dish. The seeds made into a tea increase the milk supply in nursing mothers, have a sedative effect, aid digestion, and prevent infant colic.

Fennel tea is said to be particularly good for the eyes, either by using the tea as a compress or merely by drinking it regularly. Fennel tea also has a gentle laxative effect. To prepare steep 1 teaspoon seeds in 1 cup of boiling water until desired strength is reached. It is not necessary to strain.

The licorice flavor of the fennel seed is particularly attractive to children; try giving your child branches of fennel or a few seeds to chew on rather than the usual sugary licorice candy. Or chew it yourself—it sweetens the breath. A fennel branch placed under your next loaf of Italian bread as it bakes will impart a delicious subtle flavor.

FENNEL BREAD

¼ c. lukewarm water
2 packages fresh yeast
  (or 2 tbsp. dry)
2 tsp. honey
1½ c. lukewarm water

2 tbsp. melted lukewarm
  butter
3½ c. unbleached white
  bread flour, sifted
1 tsp. fennel
1½ tsp. salt
Cornmeal

GLAZE

1 egg yolk
2 tsp. milk

4 tsp. fennel seed

Pour water over yeast and add ¼ teaspoon honey. Let it sit until the yeast begins to foam. Add lukewarm

water, 2 teaspoons honey, and melted lukewarm butter.
Stir in flour, fennel, and salt; mix well with a spoon
or hands. Turn out onto floured board and knead for
about 10 minutes. Use more flour if necessary. Put into
a large buttered bowl and cover with a towel. Let rise
about 45 minutes or until double in bulk. Punch down
and knead for 5 minutes. Shape into 2 round loaves.
Place on a cookie sheet sprinkled with cornmeal. Cover
and let rise for ½ hour. Brush with glaze of egg yolk
beaten with milk; sprinkle on 4 teaspoons fennel seed.
Bake at 350 degrees for 45 minutes or until brown.

FENUGREEK SEED Fruit of an herb native to the
Mediterranean region, fenugreek seeds are most commonly used
as tea for the relief of fever or to sooth irritated intestinal tracts.
The tea can also be used as a gargle for sore throats. One teaspoon seeds steeped in 2 cups boiling water will yield a delicate
brew with a slightly licorice flavor. In India fenugreek seeds are
used in curry sauces and the herb itself is eaten as a vegetable.
The ground seeds can be mixed with water to a gelatinous paste
and used for a poultice on wounds or inflamed areas of the skin.
In the sixteenth century it was said that the aroma of the seeds
kept away "noisome worms and creeping things."

FIG The fig is a highly perishable fruit. Unless you live in
a warm climate where figs flourish, you are likely to meet it
most often in dried form. This wholesome practical food has
been a staple for thousands of years. The Old Testament men-
tions it often and favorably, and it was a mainstay of the armies
of the Roman Empire.

Figs are extremely rich in minerals. Their iron content makes
them a good blood builder and useful in cases of anemia. Figs
are also very effective as a laxative; but if your gastrointestinal
tract is delicate, avoid this remedy, for the hundreds of tiny
seeds in each fig are indigestible and can be irritating. Dried
figs are an excellent candy substitute for children. Best results
are derived if you start giving figs as snacks at a very early age,
before the child begins to have preconceived ideas about what a
sweet should look and taste like.

Whether you buy the common black fig or the more exotic

tan type, just make certain that sulphur has not been used to speed up the drying and preserve color and that the fig has not been dipped in sugar (to sweeten it) or water (to make it weigh more and seem more moist). Properly dried figs have no need of these unhealthful and dishonest methods.

FILBERT The filbert and hazelnut belong to the same genus and the distinctions between them are so minor that they can be used interchangeably. The filbert is said to ripen on August 22, which is St. Philbert's Day . . . whence cometh the name of the nut. Filberts are small nuts with a smooth brown shell that yields easily to a nutcracker; there is no excuse for buying them preshelled! They are crisp, compact, and utterly delicious. Rich in protein and unsaturated oil, they pack such a lot of nutrition into a small space that they should be eaten in moderation. Add filberts to muesli cereal, cookies, and tortes.

FILBERT TORTE

4 eggs, separated
1 c. plus 2 tbsp. sugar
  (preferably "raw"
  sugar)

Rind of 1 lemon, grated
3 c. ground filberts

Beat egg yolks until they are foamy. Pulverize the sugar in a blender, mix with lemon peel, then beat into the egg yolks until very light. Beat egg whites in a separate bowl until they are stiff but not dry. Stir 4 tablespoons of the beaten egg whites gently into egg yolk mixture. Fold the ground nuts (2 cups shelled filberts ground in a blender will yield the 3 cups ground nuts called for) into the egg whites, then fold the whites and nuts into the egg yolks. Pour into an oiled and floured 9-inch springform pan. Bake at 350 degrees for 40–50 minutes until golden. Cool before removing from pan.

FLAXSEED Flax has been cultivated since Stone Age times for the sake of its fibrous stems, which are used to make ropes and cloth. Until the eighteenth century, when cotton came to the forefront, flax was the most important vegetable fiber in the Western world. It is now grown primarily for use in the manufacture of luxury linen materials. And for its seeds and their oil.

The seeds of the flax plant are also known as linseed, and their oil is always called linseed oil. The brown shiny seeds were once used as a food item in the Middle East (where they were often eaten roasted), and we in this country are rediscovering their nutritional worth. High in unsaturated fatty acids, protein, phosphorus, niacin, and iron, flaxseeds are said to be particularly good for dry brittle hair. Sprinkle the ground seeds on cereal, yogurt, or cottage cheese (they have a pleasant nutty flavor) and you may see your hair become thick and glossy in a matter of a few weeks. Flaxseeds are also good for constipation, as they swell and provide bulk for the intestines. Flaxseeds can be bought whole and ground into meal in a blender, or purchased preground; the meal should always be refrigerated.

Tea made from the seeds is said to be good for bronchial conditions and to have a laxative and soothing effect on the intestinal tract: Steep a tablespoon of flaxseeds in 2 cups boiling water for 15 minutes. Flaxseeds are very mucilaginous; a warm poultice made from the boiled seed or meal soothes sores, boils, and inflammations.

FLOUR   See individual flours, i.e., *Rye, Whole Wheat*, etc.

FO-TI-TIENG   Fo-ti-tieng, a member of the carrot family, is a low-lying herb that grows in the Eastern tropics. Proclaimed, like ginseng, to be a wondrous elixir, it is said to prolong life and vitality. One of its foremost exponents, Li Chung Yun, died in China in 1933 and was believed to have been 256 years old.

Fo-ti-tieng is usually available in tablet form, and as powder to be used as a tea.

FRUITS AND VEGETABLES, FRESH ORGANIC   The story of organic fresh fruits and vegetables, as available to us as buyers through commercial channels, is at the same time both hopeful and discouraging, and its development is fraught with many risks. On the one hand, more and more farmers are becoming aware of the long-run deleterious effects on their land of chemical fertilizers and pesticides and are swinging over to organic methods of farming; and these are not mere backyard gardeners but large-scale growers. This is great news for those of us who like our fruits and vegetables pure, fresh, and tasty, for it means that sky-high organic-produce prices will gradually become lower and that there will be more things organic for everyone.

On the other hand, however, the picture is not so promising. For many growers and distributors are "going organic," not through any inner conviction of the rightness of the method, but plainly and clearly to make a fast buck. They recognize the moneymaking potential of the health food boom and have no qualms about capitalizing on it. Many of the fruits and vegetables that show up for sale in the health food stores are not organic. And who is to blame? The health food store proprietor may be buying the produce in all good faith from an organic food distributor, who may in all good faith be buying it from an unscrupulous farmer who wants to make money on his pesticide-laden green-picked produce. Or an unscrupulous distributor may be buying nonorganic produce at low prices, and unknown to the farmer, the store owner, and you and me, selling it at high organic prices. Or an unscrupulous health food store owner may be going to the local supermarket, repackaging its low-priced produce, and tripling the price. Does this all sound hopelessly discouraging? Well it almost is.

What to do about it? First, try to buy fruits and vegetables that are in season in the area in which you live. They are more likely to be fresh-picked and there is often direct contact between farmer and store owner that rules out the problems of a middleman distributor. Also the sources will probably be nearby, and you can visit them and satisfy yourself as to their integrity and quality. Of course there are many items that we have grown accustomed to eating that can never be local—bananas, or citrus fruit and avocados if you live in New York. Here you have to depend on knowing and trusting your health food store owner and making sure that he is aware of the potential pitfalls in organic produce distribution and doing his utmost to avoid them.

One might well wonder whether in the end it is worth all the time and money to buy organic fruits and vegetables. Often the flavor of a well-grown tomato or orange is so superlative that it seems worth any amount of trouble and money to obtain it. Other times, however, you will find yourself with an organically raised bunch of spinach or celery that frankly just does not taste *that* much different from its chemically raised counterpart. And then the natural reaction is to beat it fast back to the supermarket and its easier prices. En route, however, remember that you will then be feeding yourself and your family any one of some forty-two chemicals that the United States Department of Agriculture has deemed "safe," to a certain level of tolerance. Often this level is passed, but only occasionally are foods officially detected and recalled. The supermarket produce is also likely to be gassed to hasten "ripening," to be dyed, soaked in antibiotic fluids to delay ripening, packed in wrappings treated with toxic materials to prevent rotting—in addition to all the pesticides that cannot be washed or peeled off, for they penetrate through the roots to the very heart of the matter.

Enough to make you scurry back to the health food store. With all its potential faults, at least there you have a chance.

A last note on organically raised fresh produce: Take the occasional worm hole as evidence of a healthful upbringing. Do not demand chemically-induced perfect appearance in organic fruits and vegetables; but do always insist on freshness.

GARLIC Garlic is a bulbous plant related to the onion; it has a strong (and to the garlic enthusiast, irresistible) odor and flavor. Miraculous healing and health-giving powers have been attributed to, garlic since Babylonian times. The wandering Israelites mourned the cherished garlic they had left behind in Egypt. It was a mainstay in the diet of the builders of the pyramids, and of ancient Greek and Roman soldiers and sailors—no Phoenician would set sail without a healthy store of garlic on board. In medieval times garlic was burned to disinfect houses visited by the plague and to ward off sickness in general.

Garlic is useful in the relief of bronchial coughs, asthma, and head colds; prepare a syrup of garlic juice and honey and take as needed. For braver types, garlic can be eaten raw; for the more reticent sufferer, garlic pills are available in health food stores. Garlic is an excellent stimulant to digestion and has an antiseptic action on the intestines. Its antiseptic qualities are also useful externally; poultices made of crushed garlic are recommended for everything from smallpox and whooping cough to poison ivy and pimples. In the Second World War the British are said to have successfully used quantities of fresh garlic to prevent infection and hasten healing of soldiers' wounds. Garlic is recognized as a laxative and is said to prevent intestinal gas.

If you like to chew garlic—this is reputed to give the most beneficial results—follow it down with some parsley or mint or fennel seeds, if you respect the noses of those around you. Garlic can be used for cooking in a myriad of manners: Chop it, crush it, squeeze it, use it whole, or merely rub it. Squeezing it through a garlic press gives the most pungent result, so restrict the amount you use accordingly. For the most subtle effect rub the cut end of the clove on bread, meat, the salad bowl.

GINGER Ginger has long been cultivated in tropical Asia. Marco Polo reported it growing in China, and Europeans raced over the "spice routes" to obtain this aromatic delicacy. It is now also grown in Africa, South America, and the West Indies. Its shallow-growing rhizome is the valued part, which we know as the ginger root. The tea, made from fresh or dried diced root of ginger, is a good tonic for digestion, delayed menstruation, nerves, and nausea. Sweetened with honey and with a slice of lemon added, it is a spicy pleasant brew. Add a few bits of ginger to a pot of chamomile tea for a real treat. Small pieces of ginger may be chewed as an aid to digestion—but these are hot on the tongue!

Try adding ½ teaspoon thin-sliced ginger root to butter before pouring in the eggs for scrambling, or a teaspoonful to your rice as it cooks for a delicate mysterious flavor. Powdered ginger is used most often in curries and cookies—and of course in gingerbread and gingersnaps.

Why not make your own ginger ale? Without harmful sugars and preservatives, you will have this delicious drink as it once was and should be.

71

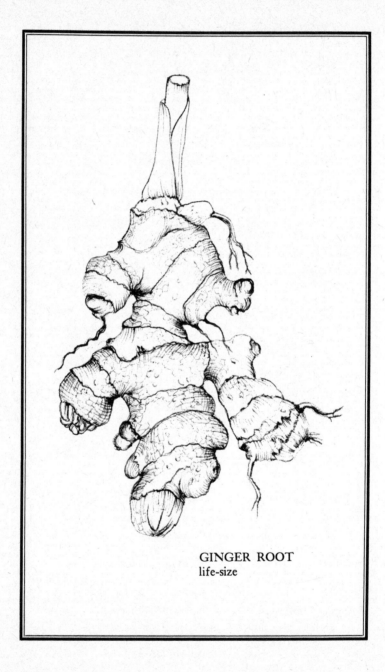

GINGER ROOT
life-size

GINGER ALE

Rind of 4 lemons (or-
    ganic, undyed if
    possible)
2 qt. water

1 c. chopped fresh ginger
    root, unpeeled (or
    reconstituted from
    dried root)
6 tbsp. honey
Juice from 4 lemons
Mint

Cut lemon rind in paper-thin strips. Pour boiling water over the chopped ginger and lemon rind; steep for 5 minutes. Strain and stir in the honey. Chill. Add lemon juice, ice, and sprigs of mint. Serves eight.
Note: For carbonated ginger ale, steep ginger and lemon peel in only 1 quart boiling water. When serving, add 1 quart cold soda water.

GINSENG Miraculous curative powers are attributed to the ginseng plant, which has held a leading position in Chinese herbal medicine for over fifty centuries. The root of the plant is the most valued part (although the leaves and flowers can be used for tea that echoes the qualities of the root, in milder form). The root is gnarled and strangely shaped, and the more it resembles the shape of a man, the more valuable it is considered. Perfect roots of this type sell for thousands of dollars on the ever-fluctuating ginseng market. Ginseng was discovered growing wild in America in the eighteenth century. Although American ginseng is considered to be inferior in quality to the Asiatic, when one considers the high prices of Asiatic ginseng, the American plant begins to look pretty good! The root has been brought under cultivation on both sides of the earth, but the cultivated root is considered inferior to the wild root.

What does it do, this magic root? Its most publicized attribute is its power to rejuvenate male sexuality (no one ever seems to say whether women might not also look to ginseng!). It is also used as a disease preventative, to aid digestion and strengthen the stomach, to promote appetite, to ward off constipation—and as a general tonic for just about any complaint in men, women, and children.

Ginseng is sold in liquid, powder, capsule, and root forms. The liquid and powder may be dissolved and taken as tea or mixed with other beverages. The root may be chewed or chopped and boiled for use as a tea.

GLUTEN FLOUR Gluten flour is wheat flour with the starch removed. It is used for bread-making by those who wish to restrict their carbohydrate intake. It can also be used to make gluten dishes, which are high in protein and therefore useful in vegetarian diets.

Gluten is an elastic protein substance that is present in all wheat flours to a greater or lesser degree. Spring or hard wheat is high in gluten, and this is what makes it a good flour for bread making; the gluten surrounds the bubbles of fermenting yeast and yields light airy loaves. Winter wheat or all-purpose flour is rather low in gluten and therefore does not lend itself to bread-making, for the loaves would be crumbling and heavy. Gluten flour comes in handy when using flours that are low in gluten, such as corn, soy, rye, oat, and barley; for each cup of a low-gluten flour, add ½ cup gluten flour in exchange for an equal amount of wheat flour, and your loaves will avoid the heaviness that these low-gluten flours tend to produce.

To make gluten for vegetarian dishes, mix gluten flour or wheat flour with water into a stiff dough; soak and knead in cold running water until the water is clear of starch and all that is left is a glutinous ball of dough. Of course this is a quicker process with gluten flour than with wheat flour. The dough is sliced and steamed or parboiled, then treated like a slice of meat to be sautéed or ground and shaped into patties or loaves.

Although gluten has the advantages of being high in protein and low in carbohydrates, it is also low in minerals—they are lost during the soaking process of extracting the gluten from the wheat flour.

GLUTEN-SOY BREAD

1 tbsp. yeast, dried (or 1 yeast cake)	1 tsp. salt
1½ c. lukewarm water	1½ c. gluten flour
1 tbsp. honey	¾ c. soy flour
1 tbsp. vegetable oil (preferably pressed oil)	¾ c. whole wheat flour

Dissolve yeast in warm water and let it rest until it begins to foam. Stir in honey and oil. Sift in salt, gluten flour, and soy flour and stir very thoroughly. Spread the whole wheat flour on a kneading board. Put batter on board, flour your hands, and knead for about 8 minutes, adding more whole wheat flour if necessary. The more you knead, the lighter the bread will be. Place it to rise in a covered oiled bowl, in a warm spot, until double in bulk; this will take an hour to an hour and a half. Then punch down the dough, form it into a loaf, and place it in an oiled bread pan. Let it rise again until the dough is just a little higher than the top of the pan. Bake in a preheated 350-degree oven for about 50 minutes. Makes one loaf.

This is a high-protein, low-starch loaf that is light and tasty—no one would ever suspect it of being a "health" bread!

GOAT MILK   Goat milk is easier for the human body to assimilate than cow milk because it contains less fat. Nearer in composition to mother's milk, it can often be tolerated by infants when cow milk is rejected. Goat husbandry has not become so industrialized as that of cows; therefore chances are that the goats will be healthier and produce milk of higher quality.

Aside from their outstanding health value, goat milk, cheese, and yogurt all have a particularly "earthy" taste that many people covet (and others abhor).

GOLDENROD TEA   When used externally this tea has a long-standing reputation for its healing power on wounds. When taken internally it has been successful with problems of the kidneys and ulcers. *Solidago odura* and *S. virgaurea* are the species of goldenrod most commonly used. One teaspoon dried flower tops should be boiled for 1 minute, steeped for 15, then strained and served. The tea has a sweet, pleasant flavor.

Goldenrod tea is sometimes also known as *solidago* tea, after the generic name for goldenrod.

GOLDEN SEAL   The medicinal properties of this wild North American plant (*Hydrastis canadensis*) lie in its bright yellow roots. It is considered to be one of our most valuable and versatile herbs. The Cherokee Indians brought it to the attention of the invading Europeans; the Indians had long valued it as a golden dye and as a veritable cure-all. Golden seal is antiseptic and can be applied externally to wounds, eczema, and poison ivy and used as an eye bath. It is laxative and functions as a bowel conditioner. It is also soothing to ulcers of the stomach and intestines and is said to relieve morning sickness during pregnancy. Applied to the gums, it will ease inflammation—but your mouth will turn bright yellow, so beware!

There is no concealing the fact that golden seal (it is sold in powder form) is extremely bitter in taste. Mix 1 to 3 teaspoons in water or orange juice, take a brave breath, and gulp it down. Best consult a homeopathic doctor for the dosage appropriate to your specific needs, for golden seal is a true medicine and not to be toyed with.

GOMASIO The macrobiotic manner of eating emphasizes the need for salt in the diet but at the same time calls for limited intake of liquid. When salt is taken in the form of gomasio, a mixture of sea salt and sesame seeds, thirst is said to be prevented. You do not have to be macrobiotic to enjoy this delicious seasoning. It is available prepared in some health food stores. Or make your own—fresh and superb.

GOMASIO

⅛ c. sea salt

1 c. raw sesame seeds,
unhulled

Grind salt into a powder with mortar and pestle (the Japanese use a special ridged ceramic bowl, a suribachi, for this). Toast the salt in a heavy frying pan until it shines; remove to another container. Roast sesame seeds in frying pan until they are lightly toasted; stir constantly with a wooden spoon to prevent burning. Grind seeds coarsely in mortar or ridged ceramic bowl; add salt and continue grinding until most—but not all— of the seeds are pulverized. The idea is for each grain of salt to be coated with sesame oil. Store in refrigerator or cool place. Use whenever salt is called for.

GRAHAM FLOUR Graham flour is a whole wheat flour made from winter wheat. Similar to whole wheat pastry flour in the fineness of its grind, it usually contains more bran. The size of the bran granules will vary from mill to mill (the making of graham flour remains an individualized process in an age of standardization!). If a recipe calls for graham flour and there is none in the cupboard, whole wheat pastry flour can be substituted, cup for cup.

The flour was named after Sylvester Graham, an American physician who in the early nineteenth century was already fighting for dietary reform. He chaffed against the horrors of useless white bread: Thousands of people "eat the most miserable trash that can be imagined, in the form of bread, and never seem to think that they can possibly have anything better, nor even that it is an evil to eat such vile stuff as they do." And our bread has certainly gone downhill even from the "vileness" of Graham's day! Graham also lent his name to the graham cracker, once a most nutritious item, now gone the way of all devitalized bakery products. Why not try stepping back in time to make your own?

GRAHAM CRACKERS

½ c. butter
⅔ c. "raw" or brown
    sugar, firmly packed
2 c. graham flour

½ tsp. salt
½ tsp. baking powder
¼ tsp. ground cinnamon
½ c. water

Cream butter and sugar well. Sift together dry ingredients and add to creamed mixture, alternating with the water. Mix well. Let stand for ½ hour. Roll out dough on floured board to ⅛-inch thickness. Cut in squares or rounds, and bake at 350 degrees on oiled cookie sheet for about 20 minutes, or until lightly browned.

GROUND IVY TEA A favorite remedy in times gone by, this bitter brew has been recommended for a variety of ailments—coughs, blood and kidney disorders, rheumatism, sciatica, gout, indigestion. The herbalist Culpepper proclaimed it "a singular herb for all inward wounds" and assured that it would expel "melancholy by opening the stoppings of the spleen."

The tonic effects of this tea may be explained by its very high mineral content. It is also rich in vitamin C and was once used by painters to prevent lead poisoning; it is now known that vitamin C combines with lead and enables it to be excreted harmlessly from the body.

Because of its bitter taste, ground ivy is usually mixed with other herb teas, such as sage, rosemary, or chamomile. Or mix it cold with orange juice. Taken cold it is an excellent bitters to stimulate the appetite.

At one time used in the processing of beer, ground ivy (*Glechoma hederacea*) is also known as gill-over-the-ground, alehoof, or gill (from the French *guiller*, to ferment beer).

GUARANA   It is rather ironical to see this substance turning up in health food stores that strictly eschew coffee and Oriental tea. For guarana contains more caffeine than any other plant—three to five times more than coffee or tea. It offers instant stimulation and will keep you awake for hours. But it has all the side effects of caffeine and an overdose can produce urinary infection. It comes from South America in a powder that looks like chocolate and is mixed with other drinks to mask its bitter taste.

HAWTHORN BERRY TEA   There are many different types of hawthorn bushes and trees throughout the temperate zones of the earth. They bear berries (or haws) that are usually red and rarely eaten by humans—though they are popular with wildlife. Some types make good jam. Hawthorn berry tea is high in vitamin C and therefore good for colds. It has also been used to alleviate heart conditions (the bark, too, is sometimes used).

The thorny hawthorn is said to have made up the crown of Christ. French peasants used to claim they could hear the hawthorn tree moan and cry on Good Fridays.

HAZELNUT   See *Filbert*.

HERBS The leaves, seeds, or flowers of various aromatic plants are known as herbs; they make of cooking an exciting adventure. Herbs can enhance or destroy a recipe. Too heavy a hand will smother all other flavors; too light a touch will leave you with boring blandness. A pinch of dried herb will go a long way; use about ⅓ as much of a dried herb as you would of a fresh one.

Fresh herbs are of course always to be preferred over dried ones, for in the drying process essential flavors are always lost to some extent. When buying dried herbs, try to find a small conscientious herb farm that treats its herbs gently and with care. Commercially dried herbs are crushed and dried on hot steel cylinders, and the heat destroys essential flavor-producing oils. Herbs distributed by large commercial concerns are also likely to have been sitting on a store shelf for untold lengths of time. Dried herbs should be used within eight months of drying, then refreshed with newly dried ones. Always store in airtight containers in a cool place—over the stove, a most handy spot, is unfortunately a bad place because the herbs get too hot.

When using herbs in cooking or in teas, remember that the strength of an herb varies greatly depending on where it is grown, when it is picked, and how it is dried. In the case of herbal teas, need we add that excess is to be avoided . . . as in everything from apples to acid.

See also individual herbs.

HIBISCUS TEA See *Karkadé Tea.*

HIZIKI This black stringlike seaweed, sometimes known as black rice, is served as a vegetable. Soak in cold water for 15 minutes, then cut into bite-size pieces, and sauté in sesame oil. Let the pan cool down, add the soaking water, and simmer for about 1 hour. This may be served alone with tamari sauce or added to any other sautéed vegetable. Like all seaweeds, hiziki is rich in iodine and trace minerals.

HONEY Honey is catching on again! After centuries of being upstaged by refined cane sugar, honey is once again coming into its own. The Greeks regarded it as food fit for gods, and men who consumed it became just a little bit godlike. Well, physiologically at any rate, we are finding that the Greeks were not far wrong. Honey is *good* for your body, and who knows, maybe for your spirit as well. Certainly there is something very comforting about a big pot full of thick amber honey sitting in the middle of a table.

Here are some of the healthful attributes of honey: It is easy on the digestive organs, for the bees have already digested it for you. It is antiseptic and gives relief to burns and skin abrasions and bee stings (yes!). As a gargle, it soothes sore throats. It is a gentle laxative. It contains many minerals, such as copper, iron, manganese, silica, chlorine, calcium, sodium, potassium, phosphorus, magnesium—dark honey is said to have a higher mineral content than light honey. Honey that has not been filtered contains vitamin C from its pollen. Chewing of the honeycomb is beneficial to sinus and hay fever congestion.

The surest way to get pure untreated, unheated honey is to buy it in the comb. Next best, try to get honey that is unfiltered (it will still be cloudy with healthful pollen) and unheated (the minerals will remain intact). Fortunately bees do not have a high resistance to insecticides; when exposed they usually die rather than carry the poison back to the hive—hard on the poor bees but fortunate for the human beings. As can be expected these days, however, many unhealthful practices have invaded the business of beekeeping. Honey is often subjected to high heat to prevent it from granulating (if your honey granulates that means it is alive and well and you only have to put it in a pot of warm water for it to liquefy again)—to all effects, it is killed. Instead of brushing the bees off the comb to extract the honey from the hive, poisons are often used to make the bees leave. Then the bees, if they live through this treatment, become weak and disease-prone and are treated with sulphur and antibiotics, which are passed on to the honey. So don't buy your honey in a supermarket. Buy from a health food store dealing with a small apiary that handles its honey ethically and with respect for this godlike substance.

Cooking with honey is unfortunately quite a problem. There are many recipes that just do not work with honey. Cookies won't be as crunchy nor cakes as light nor will preserves jell as firmly. How to get honey into your diet and sugar out? First use it in tea and coffee and on cereal and toast. Then start introducing it into your cooking. Bread accepts honey nicely; substitute it for the white sugar called for. When using honey in desserts, avoid types such as buckwheat and heather that have strong flavors—the milder the better, so that the honey will remain merely a sweetener and not submerge the taste of the dessert. A general rule of thumb is to substitute ¾ of the amount of sugar called for with honey (i.e., in a recipe calling for 1 cup of sugar, use ¾ cup honey and eliminate the sugar), and cut down the liquid in the recipe by ⅕. If you are doubtful about going all the way with honey in a certain batch of cookies, try using half sugar and half honey—you'll have the best of both worlds. Remember that every time you think of a way to use honey instead of sugar you have done your body a big favor.

HONEY-YEAST ROLLS

*1 package fresh yeast (or
   1 tbsp. dry)
¼ c. warm water
1 c. milk
¼ c. butter
⅓ c. honey*

*1 tsp. salt
2½ c. whole wheat flour,
   sifted
2½ c. unbleached white
   flour, sifted
2 eggs, well beaten*

Dissolve yeast in warm water. Scald milk and add butter and honey. Let butter melt. Cool milk mixture to lukewarm temperature and add to yeast and water; add salt and 3 cups flour. Mix well and add beaten eggs. Add rest of flour. Mix well with spoon or hands for 5 minutes. Knead until satin smooth. Place in buttered bowl; cover and let rise for about 50 minutes or until double in bulk. Punch down dough and form into round balls about the size of a golf ball. Place separately on a buttered cookie sheet or close together in a round pan that has been buttered. Cover and let rise again for about ½ hour. Bake at 375 degrees for 20 minutes or until nicely browned.
Makes about 32 rolls. Delicious served hot or rewarmed, for dinner or breakfast. These freeze well, too.

ACORN SQUASH WITH HONEY

2 *medium acorn squash*	4 *tsp. sherry (or dry*
4 *tbsp. honey*	*vermouth)*
4 *tsp. butter*	*Salt and pepper*

Preheat oven to 400 degrees. Cut each squash in half,
remove seeds, and place the 4 halves in a baking dish
filled with ½ inch water. Put 1 tablespoon honey,
1 teaspoon butter, and 1 teaspoon sherry in the center
of each piece. Sprinkle with salt and freshly ground
pepper; bake for 40 minutes or until tender when
pricked with a fork.   Serves four.

CRANBERRY SAUCE

1 *box cranberries (4 c.)*	⅛ *tsp. allspice, ground*
¾ *c. honey*	*Juice and chopped pulp*
1 *tsp. cinnamon, ground*	*of 2 medium oranges*
½ *tsp. nutmeg, ground*	½ *tsp. lemon juice*

Mix all ingredients in a saucepan and cook covered
until the cranberries are very tender—about 45 minutes.
Serve well chilled with fowl.

HOPS TEA   Although hops may be best known as an
ingredient of beer, if you are feeling nervous and sleepless then
perhaps what you need is a hot cup of hops tea, and then to
sleep on a hops pillow. Hops is a perennial vine that came by
way of China to Europe and America. Its conelike fruit is used
for beer-making; or chopped, as a nervine tea—or as a pillow
stuffing! Such pillows gained popularity after George III of
England announced that cares of state vanished with a sound
night's sleep on a mound of hops.

The tea, which is quite bitter, is above all esteemed for its
sedative and tranquilizing properties. It is also useful in cases of
indigestion, neuralgia, and liver ailments. Purportedly it will
also help to subdue sexual desire, should that be one of your
problems. The tea can be used as a poultice to ease external
inflammations, as well. To brew hops tea, steep 1 teaspoon hops
in 1 cup boiling water for about 15 minutes.

HOREHOUND TEA   The leaves of this herb of the

mint family are covered with a white hoary felt—hence its popular name, horehound. The bitter spicy leaves have long been used as a remedy for colds, coughs, and asthmatic conditions. Strong infusions of this herbal tea are diuretic and laxative —so if it's a cold you have, don't make the tea *too* strong. For coughs—both child and adult—steep a tablespoon of crushed horehound leaves in 2 cups boiling water for 20 minutes; add honey and take as needed.

Horehound candy is good for scratchy throats. Make certain, however, to purchase it sweetened with honey rather than sugar.

HORSERADISH The root of this perennial herb may cause your tongue to burn and your eyes to sting—but what a delicious taste! Horseradish originated in eastern Europe, but it is now grown and eaten in almost all parts of the world. Grated and mixed with vinegar and salt, it is the traditional accompaniment for boiled meats, tongue, and corn beef. Added to cream sauces and mayonnaise, it is a fitting partner to all sorts of fish dishes. When buying prepared horseradish, be careful that it is without noxious additives; study the labels.

Horseradish is extremely rich in vitamin C and also contains a large amount of potassium. It is diuretic, stimulates the appetite, and aids digestion. Its high content of mustard oil makes it a potential irritant to the digestive organs; if yours are weak, go easy with this herb. It will help to dissolve phlegm in the throat: Mix 1 teaspoon horseradish with 1 teaspoon lemon juice and take a couple of times a day. Horseradish mixed with vinegar was once used to make freckles fade away. But freckles are fashionable now, aren't they?

HUCKLEBERRY TEA The huckleberry bush is hardly distinguishable from its botanical relative, the blueberry, and the medicinal values of the two teas are identical. In ancient times both the berries and the leaves were infused; now only the leaves are used to make a tea that is an astringent in cases of diarrhea and is said to be useful in the treatment of diabetes because of its inulin content. To brew tea, steep 1 teaspoon leaves in 2 cups boiling water for 20 minutes.

IRISH MOSS Irish moss, also known as carrageen, is a seaweed that is very high in calcium and iodine. It is most commonly used as a thickening agent, in the same manner as agar-agar, flour, or arrowroot starch. Carrageen is one of the few emulsifying agents found in industrialized foods that is beneficial to health. Powdered Irish moss is traditionally used to make the famous blancmange and is a useful jelling agent in other custards and puddings.

Irish moss tea is made by steeping the dried moss in boiling water; strain and add honey for a brew that is helpful in cases of diarrhea and for kidney and bladder problems.

BLANCMANGE

¾ c. Irish moss	½ tsp. lemon or pure
4 c. milk	vanilla extract
Dash of salt	Honey and cream or fruit

Soak moss in cold water 5 minutes. Drain and tie moss in cheesecloth. Put in top part of double boiler with the milk and salt. Put over boiling water and cook, covered, 30 minutes. Remove bag and discard. Add flavoring to milk mixture, pour into bowl and chill until firm. Serve with honey and cream. Makes 4 servings.

JUICE, FRUIT AND VEGETABLE Fruit and vegetable juices provide valuable nutrients in an easily assimilated form. The only trouble is, through processing and storage their health value is severely impaired. Commercial juices are usually made from the frozen concentrate of insecticide-sprayed fruits and vegetables, preservatives, artificial coloring, and water (usually *lots* of it). Health food juices are often a put-on, for many of them are not made from fresh produce but from concentrate; and they have to undergo heating, which destroys nutrients (any fresh juice will start to ferment unless it is treated by heating and/or preservatives).

The best way to obtain full benefit from your juice is to invest in a juicer and make your own. A juicer is an expensive item but well worth it to those who become hooked on the joys of fresh juice. Then any combination of fruits and vegetables that hits your fancy or your nutritional needs can be made on the spot. Try mixing apple, carrot, and celery; watercress, cabbage, and celery; cucumber, lettuce, and carrot; apple and potato (all the starch remains in the pulp and its juice is rich in vitamin C); add bean sprouts to any concoction for vitamin C and minerals. Fresh juices should be enjoyed immediately after making, for they quickly lose nutrients, even under refrigeration.

JUNIPER BERRY The bluish-gray berry—fresh or dried—of the juniper evergreen tree (*Juniperis communis*) may be used for making a tea that is said to be good for kidney and bladder trouble. Used as a spray, juniper tea is said to fumigate sick rooms; and as a gargle, to prevent catching a disease to which you have been exposed. To prepare the tea steep 1 teaspoon berries in 1 cup boiling water for 2 to 4 minutes. Strain and serve.

The juniper berry is also a gourmet cooking item. Its flavor is strong and pungent and a few berries will carry you a long way. Juniper berries complement most meat dishes and are used in stuffings for everything from Cornish game hen to goose. A half-dozen berries dropped into your rice pot will make a flavorful accompaniment to a dinner of game. They are also used in meat marinades—if soaked too long they begin to have a strong resemblance to their most famous offspring, gin.

KAFFIR TEA Kaffir tea is from South Africa and is said to be made from the dried leaves of the Rooibusch shrub. It purports to taste (this is definitely a matter of opinion) and look (it does) like orange pekoe tea, but without the disturbing effects of caffeine. When steeping this tea, try adding a few pieces of lemon rind, a cinnamon stick, and several cloves; strain and add honey if desired.

KARKADE TEA A favorite drink from North Africa made from a type of hibiscus, this brilliant red drink has a flavor that is similar to lemon and is delicious served hot or cold. Use 1 teaspoonful tea to 1 cup briskly boiling water and steep for only a few minutes. Strain and serve in glasses so that you can enjoy the rich color. Karkadé combines very well with rose hips; try mixing the two for a delicious tea.

K A S H A   See *Buckwheat*.

K E F I R   Kefir is a delicious fermented milk. It is similar in taste to yogurt, and some people consider it more nutritious. It is certainly easier to make, for the milk does not have to be heated and the temperature does not have to be controlled. Kefir grains are available in health food stores, with instructions for home kefir-making.

Kefir has long been used in Eastern Europe, the Middle East, and parts of Asia. Persian women drank kefir to keep their complexions fresh and clear. It is said to be useful for inflammatory conditions of the stomach, intestinal tract, and liver. In the same way as yogurt, its friendly bacteria do away with unfriendly bacteria in the intestines. Kefir is helpful in curing both constipation and diarrhea; fresh kefir should be taken for constipation and kefir more than four days old will prove helpful with diarrhea.

K E L P   Kelp is a brown seaweed that is available in dried, powdered, or tablet form. It contains an enormous number of minerals that are extremely important to our bodies. The best known is iodine, followed by chlorine, copper, zinc, potassium, iron, sodium, magnesium, manganese, and others. The better the seawater (a sorry problem today) the better the kelp. A great deal of kelp is eaten in Japan where thyroid or goiter problems are rare due to the high intake of iodine in the seaweed. Kelp is often prescribed for the overweight, as it is said to reduce fat without harm to the body. It must be noted, however, that this takes place over a long period of time and instant results should not be looked for.

Granular or powdered kelp may be added to bread or any baked goods (half a teaspoon to a cup of flour—and eliminate the salt—is a good start). It can also be sprinkled on cheese, salad, soup, vegetables, or in juice. It has a salty flavor and can be used as a salt substitute. Kelp tablets should be taken as prescribed by your nutritionist. Dried kelp can be diced and added to soups and stews.

KIDNEY BEAN This hard red kidney-shaped bean is rich in protein and vitamin B. There are white beans of similar shape that also fall under the same name but are sometimes called marrow or cannellini beans. The nomenclature of beans is intricate! Try mixing the white with the red in this picturesque cold salad. See also *Beans, Dried*.

KIDNEY BEAN SALAD

2 c. cooked red kidney beans	1 medium-size red onion, finely chopped
2 c. cooked white kidney beans	16 artichoke hearts

Cook the beans in separate pots; otherwise the white ones will catch a dingy hue from the red. Mix the cooked and cooled beans, chopped onion, and artichoke hearts. Toss in a dressing of:

3 tbsp. olive oil (preferably pressed oil)	1 clove garlic, chopped
1 tbsp. lemon juice or vinegar	1 tsp. dried oregano
	½ tsp. dill weed
	Salt and pepper to taste

When well mixed, refrigerate for at least 3 to 4 hours. Serves four to six, depending on how big a part the salad plays in your meal.

KOMBU Although this seaweed (a type of kelp) grows in American waters, the kombu commercially available today comes from the Hokkaido Islands in Japan. It is a very healthful plant, full of iodine and other minerals. It comes in thick green sheets that must be soaked before cooking, then cut into strips. Sauté with vegetables, add to soups, or sauté alone with tamari soy sauce as a seasoning.

KUZU ROOT This tuberous root (also known as Kuzu arrowroot) is grown in remote mountains of Japan, and is supposed to have healthful qualities that tropical arrowroot lacks. Like arrowroot, it is ground into a white powder and used as a thickener of sauces, soups, and gravies. Taken medicinally as a beverage, it is said to be an energizer and to give relief from colds and diarrhea. It is much more expensive than tropical arrowroot.

LECITHIN   Lecithin has long been used by the candy and baking industries as an emulsifier and a preservative. Only rather recently has lecithin attained its present position in health food circles as a kind of wonder substance. Certainly the list of ailments it claims to cure (apparently with good justification) is impressive. It is said to reduce the cholesterol level in the body, to help eliminate liver spots, to be beneficial in cases of dry skin and psoriasis, to stimulate sexual vigor, to aid in some cases of arthritis, to stimulate brain activity, and so on. Quite enough to send one dashing out for a bagful of lecithin granules!

Lecithin is found in all nonhydrogenated oils, egg yolks, liver, brains, and soy beans. It occurs in conjunction with that oft-discussed substance, cholesterol, and seems to be essential to its proper absorption. For it is far more important to absorb the cholesterol ingested than to try to bar cholesterol from one's diet. If you use hydrogenated oils—this includes commercial peanut butter and *all* margarines—or like to savor the fat on your steak and lamb chops, best to add some lecithin to your diet. The need for lecithin increases with age.

Lecithin used to be extracted from egg yolks; now it is most commonly taken from the soybean. It is available in granules that can be used like wheat germ or added to soups and stews and baked goods. One or 2 teaspoons a day is a usual dosage. Added to bread and other baking, it will act as a preservative: substitute one-third of the oil called for in any recipe with lecithin, at the rate of 1 tablespoon lecithin to 2 tablespoons oil.

LENTIL, BROWN   One of the oldest of the leguminous plants, the humble lentil was cultivated by the ancient Egyptians and the Greeks. The lentil grows in pods like its botanical cousin the pea—there are two lentils in each small pod—and has long been known as a food of the poor people, for it offers its high protein far more cheaply than the rich man's beef. As a meat substitute, lentils are a valuable food in vegetarian diets, and in Catholic countries are much used during Lent. The protein contained in lentils, however, is not complete; therefore a meal of lentils should also include some other source of protein —perhaps a sprinkling of nuts, hard-boiled eggs, or a little cheese. The husk of the lentil seed is sometimes rather difficult to digest, but this can be overcome by adequate cooking or by straining or blending the cooked lentils. It is said that the gas-producing tendencies of lentils are lessened if they are eaten with fruits or vegetables.

COLD LENTIL SALAD

2 medium onions,
    chopped
2 cloves garlic, chopped
4 tbsp. olive oil (prefer-
    ably pressed oil)

2 c. dry lentils
4 whole cloves
2 bay leaves
Salt and pepper to taste
Water to cover

Sauté onion and garlic in olive oil until transparent. Add remaining ingredients and simmer until lentils are *just* cooked—do not overcook. Drain, remove cloves and bay leaf, and cool. Then toss lentils in 7 tbsp. olive oil (preferably pressed oil) and 3 tbsp. vinegar.

DRESSING

½ c. Italian parsley,
    chopped
1 large onion, chopped
1 tbsp. mustard

Juice of 1 lemon
Salt and pepper
Olive oil (preferably
    pressed oil)

Mix above ingredients, except for olive oil. Slowly add oil until dressing thickens. Add to lentils and mix well. Garnish with watercress and tomato wedges.

LENTIL, RED The famed red pottage for which Esau sold his birthright was most likely made from the Egyptian red lentil. Today these tiny orange-red beans are also cultivated in northern France and are greatly valued for their delicate flavor. In Scotland the red lentil is also often used, and is sometimes known as "Scottish cereal."

Red lentils have a more subtle flavor than their stalwart brown confreres. They cook quickly without presoaking, and can be used in soups, stews, and Indian *dal*.

DAL

2 tbsp. butter	½ tsp. chile pepper
1 large onion, chopped	1 tsp. cumin powder
1 tsp. salt	1 tsp. ground coriander
2 tsp. turmeric	2 c. boiling water
2 tbsp. ginger powder	1 c. red lentils
(or 1 tbsp. fresh	
chopped root)	

Sauté in butter all ingredients except lentils. When onions are soft, add 2 cups boiling water and the washed lentils. Lower heat and simmer covered for 20 minutes or until lentils are tender. More water may be added if a thinner sauce is desired. This dish will burn easily, so use a heavy pot and watch it carefully.

Serve alone or as a sauce over rice, bulgur, or kasha. No proper Indian meal is ever complete without its *dal*.

LICORICE ROOT   The rhizomes and roots of this perennial herb have been used since ancient times. Their sweet pungency has been extracted for the making of beverages, candies, and pastries. Try giving a child a piece of licorice root to chew on instead of the artificially sweetened conglomeration that now bears the name of licorice.

As a medicinal, licorice root gives relief from sore throats and coughs. It is often an ingredient in throat lozenges. Add a few chips off a licorice root to some rose hips, and you will have a delicious tea that is extremely good for colds. Licorice has a laxative tendency.

LINDEN TEA   The sweet-scented flowers and heart-shaped leaves of this tree have made it a symbol of love and a poetic subject for generations. The linden is also known in the

LICORICE ROOT
life-size

United States as basswood. Both the flowers and the leaves are used in making a medicinal tea. Boil together in water, then strain and use either hot or cold. This infusion is very useful in promoting perspiration and is a good remedy for coughs and vomiting.

LINSEED OIL Linseed oil is expressed from the linseed or flaxseed. When cold-pressed, it is relatively odorless and tasteless and may be used for cooking and salads. Widely used as a medium by painters and for the making of paints, varnishes, and linoleum, the commercial oil is extracted by use of high heat and IS NOT SUITABLE FOR HUMAN CONSUMPTION.

LIVER, DESICCATED Desiccated liver tastes *awful*! But its health benefits are so tremendous that many many people are more than willing to put up with the taste. It is a high-energy, iron-rich food that contains the whole vitamin B complex, lots of vitamin A, copper, calcium, phosphorus, and protein. Desiccated liver is made by drying beef liver (try to find an organic source, made from liver without pesticide residues) at very low temperatures in order to preserve the highest amount of nutritional value. It can be mixed in orange juice or tomato juice—but it does not dissolve, so gulp it down fast. It can also be mixed in with your stews, hamburgers, and soups. Or you can take it in capsule form; the only trouble is, you have to take about 30 capsules to equal the amount of powder you can get down in one fell swoop in a glass of juice.

LOTUS ROOT TEA This sweet and mild tea may be made from either the fresh or dried root of the Oriental lotus. In either case it is said to be very helpful for respiratory problems. Fresh, the root is grated and boiled in an equal amount of water with a pinch of salt; strain and serve. The dry root, which is usually powdered, is prepared by mixing 1 teaspoon of the powder with 2 cups water. Simmer and just before serving add a bit of grated ginger and tamari soy sauce.

MACE As the pear-shaped fruit of the nutmeg tree splits open with ripeness, a bright red filigreed network is revealed, which encases the nutmeg kernel. This network is mace. It is carefully removed from the kernel, dried (losing its red color for a rich brown), and ground for use as a delicate culinary spice. Mace can be substituted in any recipe calling for nutmeg; the taste of the two is quite different—and yet somewhat the same. Use mace in cookies, bread, and cheese; or to add flair to rice, ground meat, and fish sauce.

It is good to remember, however, that mace in very large amounts can be dangerous.

MALVA TEA The leaves of this common wayside weed (*Malva rotundifolia* or *M. neglecta*) yield a tea that is high in vitamin A and minerals—a good tonic. The leaves also lend pungency and health to soups and salads.

It would probably not be a good idea to gorge yourself on malva leaves, however—they have been implicated in some cases of livestock poisoning.

MAPLE SYRUP, PURE   Pure maple syrup is, alas, a vanishing commodity. Imitation "pure" maple syrups abound on the markets; even those syrups claiming to contain no additives have usually been processed in a most distasteful manner. In 1962 the Food and Drug Administration sanctioned the use of formaldehyde tablets (or pellets) in the tapholes of sugar maple trees. Although this law was passed in the name of sanitation, the truth is that the tablet keeps the taphole open and allows the sap to flow much earlier and longer than it should or ever has. The supreme flavor of syrup tapped at its prime is utterly lost. As for the formaldehyde, its users claim that it evaporates as the syrup is boiled. We, however, would feel more at ease if the formaldehyde had kept its old-fashioned place on the poison shelf! Also, bacterial cultures may be added to the syrup to restore proper flavor, and antifoaming agents are often used.

In some areas of Vermont and Canada these additives and the "pellet" are not used. Know your sources and demand untreated syrup.

Yet after all is said and done, because the syrup is made by evaporation and is exposed to heat for a long period of time, the finished product is no more nor less than a delicious sugar. It would be more healthful to use unheated honey or molasses on your next batch of pancakes—but we cannot pretend that there is really any substitute for the delicate sweetness of pure maple syrup!

MAPLE MOUSSE

1 pt. heavy cream   *Pinch of salt*
¾ c. maple syrup   *¼ c. ground nuts*
6 egg yolks

Beat heavy cream until it is thick but not whipped. In a double boiler heat the syrup until it is just warm. Add well-beaten egg yolks slowly, stirring constantly. Add salt. Stir until the mixture thickens—about 3 to 4 minutes. Remove from heat and stir until it cools. Fold in the cream. Pour into one larger bowl or into individual cups and put in the freezer of your refrigerator.

Remove frozen mousse from the freezer 20 minutes
before you plan to serve it. Sprinkle ground nuts on top.
A luxuriously rich dessert.   Serves six.

MARGARINE Margarine in its "natural" form is a white
and greasy lardlike substance made from hydrogenized animal
or vegetable fat. It was originally used as an ingredient in commercial biscuitry to preserve crackers and keep them crisp for
long periods of time. Later it began to be used as an inexpensive
substitute for butter, with packets of yellow dye supplied to
the homemaker who couldn't quite stomach its waxy pallidity.
Recent food regulations have allowed margarine to be artificially colored and flavored at the factory and have counte-
nanced false advertising campaigns that tout margarine's high
content of unsaturated oils. Low-class margarine suddenly became a respected and supposedly even healthful food!
    Do not be led astray by advertising gimmickry. Realize that
for margarine to attain butterlike hardness, it has to have a high
content of hydrogenized fat—an extremely unhealthful substance that is liable to contribute to rather than alleviate cholesterol problems. This applies also to the softer whipped margarines. The small amount of unsaturated liquid oil that is added
to "health food" margarine does little to correct the situation.
Synthetic vitamin A is also added to margarine, in simulation of
butter; the natural vitamin A found in good-quality butter is far
preferable. Use margarine sparingly and read labels with care.

MARJORAM Sweet marjoram is the more restrained relative of wild marjoram (oregano). Its name derives from the
Greek for "joy of the mountain." Certainly it is a joy in the
kitchen! It is particularly good (fresh or dried) with lamb and
other meats and will lend delicious flavor to scrambled eggs and
steamed vegetables. Its flavor is more subtle than oregano's, but
it nonetheless has a pungency to be reckoned with judiciously.
    Marjoram, like many other herbs, was appreciated in pre-
refrigeration days for its disinfectant qualities. As a tea, it is
mildly tonic, but other herbs are more medicinally inclined than
this one. Its oil is used as a liniment to relieve neuralgia and
sprains. Before the days of hops it was used to brew beer and
ale.

MARJORAM OMELETTE

3 cloves garlic, chopped
¾ c. fresh parsley,
  chopped (or ⅓ c.
  dried)
3 medium onions, sliced
1 tbsp. butter
2 tbsp. olive oil (preferably pressed oil)

3 c. sliced zucchini
1 tsp. dried marjoram (or
  2 tsp. fresh)
½ tsp. salt
¼ tsp. black pepper,
  ground

Sauté garlic, parsley, and onion in butter and oil for
3 to 4 minutes—do not brown. Add zucchini,
marjoram, salt, and pepper. Cook until tender. Set aside
and keep warm while you make the omelettes. This
makes enough filling for 4 two-egg omelettes or 1
eight-egg omelette. Spoon the warm filling onto one side
of the omelettes (or omelette) while it is still in the
pan; fold in half.   Serves four.

MARSHMALLOW ROOT This geraniumlike herb
(*Althea officinialis*) grows wild along coastal salt marshes in

Europe and the United States and can also be cultivated in your garden. The name usually brings to mind the white marshmallow confection—originally made from powdered root of marshmallow; our marshmallows, however, no longer have anything whatsoever to do with this very useful herb—being made as they are of a nutritionless conglomeration of corn syrup, sugar, and gelatin.

Powdered or pounded marshmallow root can be used as a poultice to ease skin irritations such as burns, bedsores, and abrasions. The sliced root can also be boiled to make a tea; it is said to alleviate hoarseness and coughs because of its emollient qualities.

An old saying has it that the marshmallow plant will only grow near happy homes.

MARSHMALLOW TEA This tea is prepared with the leaves and flowers of the marshmallow plant (see Marshmallow Root) and has a number of beneficial uses—for lung and throat problems as well as for coughs and tender gums. It is also helpful in cases of dysentery and bowel inflammation. Applied to the eyes, the tea eases inflammation and styes; as a douche it soothes vaginal irritations. In all cases it functions, like the marshmallow root, as a softener or emollient, and as such alleviates discomfort rather than offering a cure.

To prepare the tea simply take about 2 teaspoons of leaves and/or flowers and let them steep for 10 to 15 minutes. Strain and add honey if you like.

MEAT The idea of a herd of beef cattle grazing on a grassy hillside on a warm summer day is delightful, but sadly not very realistic. Today a larger percentage of our cattle than anyone would care to admit are raised in the quickest, cheapest, least healthful, and most unnatural manner possible. Probably no food on the market is altered as much as meat. Nutrition and even the modicum of health—either of animal or of human consumer—are ignored and money is the motivation in the meat-producing business.

Most beef cattle are now conceived through artificial insemination, immediately weaned on foods loaded with drugs, pesticides, antibiotics, and synthetic vitamins (so much for the

old-fashioned virtues of mother's milk and verdant pastures!),
and finally shot full of tranquilizers and meat tenderizers before
being led to the slaughter. The woeful lives of unfortunate
pigs, veal calves, lambs, and chickens follow the same maleficent
pattern. Pigs are fed processed garbage; veal calves are kept in
a state of acute anemia and absolute immobility in order to produce pale muscleless meat; lambs may be shorn chemically, with
the chemical then penetrating into the flesh, while "spring" lamb
is now produced twice yearly by manipulating the light of an
artificial environment; chickens are raised in windowless super-
structures, with their arsenic-doused food (for more yellow
skin) passing by on conveyer belts.

Perhaps the most dangerous drug used in meat is an artificial
female hormone implanted in the neck or ear of the animal or
put into its food. This drug is called diethylstilbestrol or DES.
Its purpose is to create a heavier animal in a shorter length of
time, primarily through a buildup of excess fat—leaving you,
the consumer, to pay meat prices for contaminated fat! Diethylstilbestrol is a known carcinogen, and has been shown to
cause cancer and sterility in test animals. Nevertheless, the Food
and Drug Administration in 1970 bowed to meat industry pressure and doubled the amount of DES allowed to be fed to
cattle.* Other problems we are faced with in our meats are
coloring to make the meat look fresher longer, and chemicals
(such as nitrates and nitrites) to make it last longer without
obvious spoilage.

Unfortunately it is extremely difficult to find fresh organically
raised meat. What there is of it is usually frozen and extremely
expensive. If you are not prepared to make the leap to organic
meat, there are certain precautions that can be taken to ensure
more health and less contamination for you and your family.
Choose your butcher carefully; find out where he gets his meat
and how it has or has not been treated; watch to make sure the
ground meat is freshly ground in a well-cleaned grinder; have
as much fat as possible trimmed off the meat, for it is in the fat

---

* As this book goes to press, the Food and Drug Administration has finally
acknowledged the cancer-producing effects of diethylstilbestrol, and has
banned its use in feed as of January 1, 1973. Diethylstilbestrol pellet implants
are still allowable, however, until further FDA testing confirms the obvious
fact that they, too, are highly undesirable.

that the stilbestrol and pesticides leave a great deal of their residue. An FDA ruling forbidding implantation of stilbestrol pellets in chickens' necks is not always adhered to, so think twice before making broth with the neck. There is controversy over whether liver is still fit for human consumption. Some contend that because the liver is the body's "clearinghouse," as it were, all of the chemicals the animal has been exposed to are deposited there in concentrated form. Others claim that the health value and vitamin B content of liver are so high that liver remains one of the healthiest of meats. Take your pick. . . .

MILK, CERTIFIED RAW Certified raw milk is un-pasteurized milk that has to meet high and rigid standards of quality. The cows producing such milk must be fed fodder uncontaminated by DDT and other pesticides, regularly inspected for disease, cared for by absolutely healthy personnel, and the equipment carrying milk from cow to container must be completely sterile. These rules are strictly enforced and milk bearing the certified label is absolutely safe to drink and highly nutritious.

Pasturized milk, on the other hand, is steadily declining in nutritional value and carries in it many harmful elements. Antibiotics that are pumped into cows in pasteurized herds go straight into the milk and are not killed by pasteurization. Neither are the pesticides nor the hormones eliminated. Bacteria count is allowed to be extremely high in the belief that pasteurization will kill everything—which somehow becomes like the difference between drinking boiled contaminated water and pure spring water. Pasteurized milk is often exposed to excessively high temperatures that destroy large amounts of its calcium—(the main reason we drink milk!) and alters its nutritional content extensively.

If you cannot find certified raw milk—and it is becoming increasingly difficult to obtain in most parts of the United States, for organized dairy interests are dead set on forcing it off the market—try to buy from a local farmer whose operation you know is clean. There are still a few regional dairies around that pride themselves on a particular herd of Alderney or Guernsey cows that are thoughtfully cared for. Search them out! Then you will be getting all of the rich vitamin A and D, potassium, phosphorus, calcium, and protein that you deserve from a glass of milk.

MILK, POWDERED NONINSTANT Skim or whole noninstant powdered milk has been spray-processed at a very low temperature and its nutritional value left more or less intact. It is high in protein, calcium, and minerals. Instant powdered milk, however, is heated at extremely high temperatures and thereby loses enormously in nutritional value. Instant powdered milk is also difficult to use in cooking and cannot be added directly to recipes without detrimental effects—bread becomes leaden and yogurt stringy, to give just two examples. Noninstant powdered milk, on the other hand, adds body and nutritional value to just about anything you care to add it to—gravies, cookies, soups, bread, yogurt, etc.

Powdered milk should not, however, be considered a complete substitute for fresh milk; its composition has been altered in the drying process, and despite all its benefits, it has become an unbalanced food. But as a fortifier of other foods, it is extremely useful. Make fortified milk by adding noninstant powdered milk to regular milk at the rate of ½ cup powdered milk to 1 quart fresh milk. Remember after opening powdered milk to keep it in a tightly sealed jar; moisture can cause its bacteria content to rise.

MILLET Millet is probably one of our most ancient grains and has been used in India, Africa, and the Middle East since prehistoric times. Its name derives from the Latin *mille* (a thousand), referring to the prolificacy of the millet seed. This grain grows easily in a wide range of soils and climates, and a large variety of species fall under its name—ranging from sorghum to the small pearl-like grains that we know and eat as "common" millet.

Millet is a particularly nutritious grain, containing good amounts of iron, magnesium, potassium, and some protein. It can be used as a breakfast cereal, a rice substitute, or ground coarsely (a blender will do) and added to wheat flour for deliciously different loaves of bread.

Although millet is most commonly seen in the United States as an ingredient in birdseed mixtures, it deserves a place on your table as well.

MILLET PARMIGIANO

1 c. millet	*1 tsp. salt*
2 c. boiling water (or broth)	*3 tbsp. Parmesan cheese, grated*
2 tbsp. butter	

Toast millet in pot until it gives off a delectable nutty aroma, stirring to prevent burning. Add boiling water or broth, butter, and salt. Simmer in a covered pot for about 40 minutes or until water is absorbed and millet is fluffy. When done, fluff with a fork and sprinkle grated cheese on top. 				Serves four.

MILLET, CRACKED Cracked millet falls between whole millet and millet meal in size and can serve as a substitute for either. Used in bread instead of meal, it gives a slightly crunchy loaf. When used as a main dish or cereal instead of whole millet, it will be finer in texture and quicker cooking. Try it as a cereal with toasted sesame seeds sprinkled, and honey ribboned, generously over it. See also *Millet.*

MILLET MEAL Ancient Romans made their bread of millet meal and wheat flour. Try adding ½ cup ground millet (a blender or coffee grinder will do the trick if you cannot buy the meal commercially) per each 5 cups of wheat flour to your next batch of bread. See also *Millet.*

MINERALS Minerals are inorganic substances found in food, which are essential to human life. Ideally all the minerals we need should be obtained from the food we eat. Often, however, they are lost in cooking or were never there in the first place due to poor agricultural and processing practices. So mineral supplements are sometimes necessary. Minerals obtained from natural sources are far more easily assimilated than are chemically isolated minerals.

MINT The mint family of herbs is a large one. There are more than twenty different species of mint and hundreds of related species. Apple mint, Indian mint, bowles mint, horsemint, bergamot mint, pineapple mint, Corsican mint (which is used for making *crème de menthe* liqueur), even catnip (see *Catnip*), are a few of the many minty variations that can grow in your garden or lend aroma to your lemonade and tea. Mint is often mixed with various herbal teas to give added flavor. Peppermint tea stands on its own, with superb flavor and healthful qualities.

Spearmint and peppermint are the two most widely used types of this herb (see *Peppermint; Spearmint*).

MISO Miso is a dark soybean paste that has been aged in wooden barrels for three years. There are several types of miso: mugi, hacho, and kome. Mugi miso is for everyday use, particularly good for temperate weather, of medium strength, and made of soybeans, barley, sea salt, and water. Hacho miso is stronger in taste, good for cold weather, yang in tendency, and made from soybeans, sea salt, and water. Kome miso is the most mild in taste, particularly used in hot weather and for women and children, and is made from soybeans, brown rice, sea salt, and water.

Miso might well be called the macrobiotic's "yogurt." For it has a beneficial action on intestinal bacteria similar to the fermented milk. Miso is also very high in easily assimilated proteins. Mix 1½ teaspoons miso with a little water and add to 2 cups hot water for an invigorating broth; add it to any soup for a bouillon flavor. Take care to add miso toward the end of the cooking, however, and do not boil it or some of its healthful properties will be destroyed. Miso can be used uncooked in dips and sauces and spreads. Here is a delicious sandwich filling.

MISO BUTTER

½ c. miso   1½ c. sesame tahini
water

Mix the miso with a little bit of water to make a smooth paste. Add tahini and blend well. Very good on a slice of dark whole grain bread. This will keep a long time refrigerated.

MOLASSES When sugarcane juice is boiled down and the raw sugar extracted, a thick dark syrup remains. This is blackstrap molasses. Further refining yields a slightly paler, less strong-tasting molasses. Both are highly nutritional, particularly compared to their devitalized relative, refined sugar. Blackstrap molasses takes the lead, however, in high iron, potassium, calcium, and vitamin B content. An extremely valuable substance in the treatment of iron deficiency, low energy, constipation, and nervous strain, its taste, however, is rather overpowering; but when mixed half and half with honey and used to flavor yeast drinks, cereals, bread, milk shakes, or yogurt, it is quite palatable. Do not take it straight from a spoon; it tends to stick to the teeth and may cause decay.

GINGERBREAD MEN

⅓ c. butter	1½ tsp. baking soda
1 c. molasses	½ tsp. cloves, ground
½ c. yogurt	2 tsp. cinnamon, ground
¼ c. sugar (preferably "raw" sugar)	2 tsp. ginger, ground
	½ tsp. salt
3¼ c. unbleached white flour	

Cream butter and molasses together. Add yogurt and sugar. Sift in flour, soda, spices, and salt. Mix well; the dough will be fairly stiff. Roll out dough on a floured board and cut into gingerbread-men shapes, or form shapes with your hands without rolling out. Place on a lightly oiled cookie sheet and bake at 350 degrees for 12 to 15 minutes. Makes about two dozen.

MORROMI Morromi is a paste made of the soybean pulp that is left after the making of tamari soy souce. It is used in the same manner as miso but is quite a bit milder in flavor.

MU TEA Mu means infinity and this tea is said to lead you up the road toward infinite wisdom. However that may be, mu tea is a delicious beverage. You may want to save it for special occasions, for it is very expensive. It is a mixture of sixteen exotic herbs and seeds: ginseng, ligusticum, paonia root, cypress, orange peel, ginger, rehmannia, cinnamon, cloves, peach kernels, coptis, licorice root, cnicus, stractylis, moutan, and hoelen.

The tea comes in a small package that should be emptied into a quart of water and boiled about 20 minutes. Use an enamel pan—*never* aluminum. Strain and serve. The herbs may be saved and used one more time, but don't wait more than two days or they will lose flavor.

MUGICHA BARLEY TEA   Made from roasted unhulled grains of barley, this tea has a rather strong taste and is used by some people as a coffee substitute. Put a generous pinch in 2 cups water and boil for 20 minutes. Strain and serve.

MULLEIN BLOSSOM TEA   Make certain that your mullein blossoms are bright yellow, for therein lies their medicinal value. When carefully dried to retain their color, they can be a helpful aid against coughs, chest trouble, colds, and inflammations of the throat or mouth. Steep 2 teaspoons blossoms in 2 cups of boiling water until it reaches a summer yellow; drink as needed. Add honey for a tastier tea. The vapors of the tea may be inhaled and will relieve congestion due to colds.

Mullein blossom tea is occasionally referred to as Verbascum, the generic name of the plant from which it is prepared.

MUNG BEAN   These small green beans are grown primarily in India—from whence comes their name—but they are also cultivated on a smaller scale in many other tropical countries. In America they are most frequently used to make sprouts that are sweet and crunchy, tender enough to be used raw, and substantial enough to stand sautéing. The sprouts are highly nutritious, contain large amounts of vitamin C, and are very simple to grow. For sprouting instructions, see *Sprouts*.

MUSHROOM, DRIED   Dried mushrooms are a delectable item that should be on every kitchen's shelf. Not only are they an epicurean delight; they are also rich in B vitamins, riboflavin, potassium, phosphorus and contain vitamin D and protein. They can of course be used to replace fresh mush rooms, but the dried mushroom should also be appreciated as a food all to itself. A wide variety is available; one can savor the vivid differences between Italian, French, and Chinese fungi—whereas with fresh mushrooms we are limited to the one variety offered by commercial markets.

Dried mushrooms give excellent flavor to soups, sauces, and stews. Before using, wash them, then soak in water to cover for ½ hour. Do not throw out the brown soaking water; add it to your recipe for delicious additional flavor.

SAFFRON RICE WITH DRIED MUSHROOMS

¼ c. dried mushrooms	*¼ tsp. powdered saffron*
2 c. liquid (water or	*1½ tbsp. butter*
broth and mushroom	*½ c. grated Parmesan*
water)	*cheese*
1 tsp. salt	*Pepper to taste*
1 c. brown rice	

Wash and soak mushrooms in water to cover for ½ hour. Drain and save water. Slice mushrooms if they have become very large during soaking. Add mushroom water to broth or water to make 2 cups, add salt, bring to boil, and slowly sprinkle in rice so that boiling does not stop. Add mushrooms. Cover and simmer 40 minutes until rice is tender. Fold saffron into rice with fork until rice is evenly yellow. Then fold in butter, cheese, and pepper.   Serves four.

MUSTARD The seed of the robust mustard greens contains a volatile oil that is a delight to the tongue but a problem for the innards—too much mustard can cause inflammation of the stomach and intestines. There are two varieties of mustard seed—white (sometimes called yellow) and black; black is the stronger. Whole mustard seeds are used in pickles and relishes. Ground mustard seed is said to have originated in the eighteenth century when a fine lady of Durham, England, thought to grind the mustard seed into a powder, discarding the husk. This "Durham" mustard caught the eye of King George I, so the story goes, and thence soared to popularity. Ground mustard is now widely used in sauces, salad dressings, and cheese dishes; or as a condiment in itself, mixed with water, white wine, or beer. Of the many varieties of prepared mustards available, Dijon and Dusseldorf types are generally considered to be the finest.

As a medicinal, mustard has long been in use, having received the endorsement of Hippocrates himself. The mustard plaster, made of equal parts ground mustard, flour, and water (add an egg white and additional flour when applying to very sensitive skin), gives time-honored relief for congested lungs and muscular aches. Do not leave such a plaster on for too long or it will cause the skin to blister. A sure—and not particularly pleasant—way to induce vomiting involves gulping down a glass of warm water with a teaspoon of mustard powder dissolved in it.

ORIENTAL CHICKEN

2 tbsp. curry powder
2 tbsp. soy sauce
½ c. prepared mustard
  (Dijon is good)

½ c. mild honey
1 3-lb. chicken, cut in
  half or in pieces

Mix together curry powder, soy sauce, mustard, and honey. Spread over chicken and marinate for ½ to 2 hours. Place chicken bone side up in 350-degree oven. Cook ½ hour, then turn chicken over and baste so that a glaze will form over chicken; bake ½ hour more, or until meat is tender. Serve with rice.

Serves four.

NETTLE TEA If you have ever been stung by the prickly leaves of this wild herb, you may be reluctant to think of the nettle as a food. When dried or boiled, nettles completely lose their sting; pick them with gloves and scissors and you will be master of the situation. Boiled, they become a spinachlike vegetable, tasty and high in vitamin A, iron, and a wide variety of minerals.

Either the leaves or the roots of the common stinging nettle (*Urtica dioica*) may be used to brew a tea that has valuable powers as a tonic and blood cleanser, and it is extremely effective against kidney problems. When using dry nettle leaves, note that the greener they are, the more healthful.

A strong nettle tea, made by boiling a teaspoon of dried

leaves in 2 cups water (or vinegar) for ½ hour, is a very good hair rinse and is said to reinvigorate the hair and restore waning color. Slightly more obscure uses of nettle: Beat rheumatic or paralytic limbs with nettle branches to restore vigor and circulation (this may also call for masochistic tendencies!); spin thread from nettle stems and weave table linen, as did the Scandinavians and Scottish in times of yore.

NORI   This Japanese seaweed comes in thin sheets, which are toasted quickly over the burner of your stove, then crumbled and used as a garnish over vegetables, rice, noodles, or used as a covering for rice balls. Nori has all the healthful qualities inherent in the mineral-rich seaweed family, which is said to be particularly useful for thyroid and prostate problems and to neutralize toxic substances in the body—even the infamous strontium 90.

NUT   See also individual nuts.

Nuts are among the most nutritious of all foods. They contain relatively more protein than most other foods of plant origin and are therefore of great value as a meat substitute. They are also high in unsaturated fatty acids, B vitamins, and a multitude of minerals—phosphorus, iron, calcium, in particular. Because of this load of nutrients, nuts should be eaten sparingly and chewed well. For greatest nutritive value and easy digestibility, eat nuts in their most natural form. This means nuts in their shells; shells that have not been gassed (for easier cracking), bleached (for uniformity of appearance), or dyed (who needs purple pecans and red pistachios?).

Once the shell is removed from a nut, it will quickly grow rancid unless refrigerated. Therefore almost all shelled nuts are treated in obnoxious manners to give them indefinite shelf life, and they should be avoided if possible. When you must buy shelled nuts, purchase them at a health food store that keeps them refrigerated. Also give a wide berth to roasted nuts. These are cooked at high temperatures that destroy much of the nutritive value; they are often saturated with hydrogenized oils used in the "roasting" process; and they are usually oversalted and sometimes even sugared. Roast your own nuts; it's easy and the taste is incomparable.

ROASTED NUTS

On top of the stove: In a heavy iron skillet, place 1 to 2 cups fresh-shelled nuts. Adjust heat to medium high, and stir nuts until they begin to let off their delicious aroma (about 10 minutes)—be careful not to overroast. Sprinkle with sea salt (stir in 1 teaspoon pressed vegetable oil, and the salt will cling evenly to the nuts) if desired and serve warm.

In the oven: Place 1 to 2 cups fresh-shelled nuts on a baking sheet. Place in a 350-degree oven. Every 5

NUTMEG
Fruit (center), Seed (left),
Mace (right)–life-size
Branch and flowers–⅓ size

minutes stir the nuts. In about 15 minutes their heady aroma will let you know they are ready—be careful not to overroast. Sprinkle with sea salt if desired and serve warm.

NUTMEG Nutmeg is the seed of a small pear-shaped fruit borne by the East Indian *Myristica fragrans*—or nutmeg—tree. The same tree also produces mace, the latticed network that surrounds the nutmeg kernel, and in itself a spice.

Nutmeg is easy to grate whenever a recipe calls for it, so for the most savory results buy your nutmeg whole. Many people keep a small grater and a few nutmegs in a closed jar, handy for use. Be sure to remove any white powder that may be clinging to the surface; that is lime, which is often used to keep the nutmeg dormant and insect free—and it's not good for the stomach.

Nutmeg will enhance most any dish; try a dash in black bean soup, or on buttered vegetables, and in anything made with milk—baked custard, bread pudding, cottage cheese.

Oil of nutmeg, made by crushing the hard seed, is said to settle the stomach. A drop only, in a cup of herb tea, should do the trick. And should you yearn for a good night's sleep, try applying the fragrant oil to the temples in Oriental style as you settle into bed.

SPINACH PIE

Pie pastry to line bottom of 9-inch pan
Grated rind of ½ lemon (preferably organic and undyed)
¾–1 lb. of fresh spinach
2 tbsp. butter
3 eggs, beaten
1 c. ricotta (or small-curd creamed cottage cheese)

⅓ c. Parmesan cheese, grated
6 tbsp. cream (or milk)
½ tsp. salt
⅛ tsp. freshly ground pepper
¼ tsp. freshly ground nutmeg

Line pie pan with rolled dough to which lemon rind has been added, and bake for 10 minutes in a 375-degree oven. While this is cooking, wash and drain spinach and cook briefly in the water that clings to the leaves, just until it is wilted. Drain spinach well, chop, and mix with the butter. In another bowl beat eggs, then mix in ricotta, Parmesan cheese, cream, salt, pepper, and nutmeg. Stir in spinach and butter. Spread into the partially cooked pie shell and bake 30 minutes in 375-degree oven, until it is browned and firm to the touch. Serve warm to four to six people.

OAK BARK TEA This tea is very astringent due to its high tannin content. It is useful in cases of diarrhea and dysentery; as a gargle for swollen throats, and as a poultice for varicose veins and goiter.

OAT FLOUR Oat flour gives a moist sweetness to breads, pancakes, scones, and biscuits that is hard to match. This flour is also extremely good for the skin. Add to bath water and it will sooth the itch of irritations such as exzema, poison ivy, and poison oak. Or make a thick poultice of it and apply directly to the diseased parts. These homemade preparations are just as effective and far less expensive than commercially sold "colloidal oatmeals." Oat flour is an effective skin cleanser and can replace soap when necessary; make a paste with water and apply to the skin, then rinse off.

OAT FLOUR SCONES

1 ¾ c. oat flour	*2 tbsp. honey*
½ tsp. baking soda	*3 tbsp. sour cream*
2 tsp. baking powder	*2 tbsp. vegetable oil (or*
1 ½ tsp. salt	*melted butter)*
2 eggs	*1 tbsp. milk*

Mix together oat flour, baking soda and powder, and salt. Beat eggs, and set aside 1 tablespoon of egg to use for glaze. Stir in honey, sour cream, and oil. Add liquid mixture to dry mixture and stir well. Turn onto a board dusted with oat flour and knead briefly, using more flour if necessary. The dough will be soft and slightly sticky. Shape into a round ball. Place the ball on a lightly oiled baking sheet and pat out with hands into a smooth circle; the dough should be about ½ inch in thickness. With a knife dipped in flour or cold water, cut the circle into 8 wedges, but leave them in place. Mix the reserved tablespoon of egg with milk and brush the mixture over the scones. Bake in 350-degree oven for about 30 minutes or until nicely browned.

OAT GROATS Oat groats are the whole, uncut, uncrushed kernel of oatmeal. They can be used for cereal, but it's long cooking. They are most useful for sprouting and adding to salads and sandwiches. Oat sprouts are extremely high in vitamin B_2 and other valuable nutrients. See also *Sprouts* and *Oatmeal*.

OAT STRAW TEA The leaves or straw of the oat plant can be cut up, boiled for ½ hour, and used as a tea that is said to be tonic, soothing, and good for the heart and chest. The tea can also be added to your bath; it is good for sensitive skin.

OATMEAL Oatmeal is a catchall term for any number of different types of oats. Steel-cut oats of various grinds, rolled oats, oat flakes, oat groats, may all be referred to as oatmeal. They are simply different treatments of the oat grain, which grows worldwide in climates that are too cold for wheat. Oats possess many healthful qualities—the celebrated physique of the Scots is said to be due to its virtues.

Processed oat products retain more of their original health value than processed wheat products; for when the oat is milled the outer husk comes off but the bran and germ are left intact, unlike wheat whose commercial milling removes both bran and germ. So you will get a better nutritional deal with supermarket rolled oats than with most other supermarket-type cereals. But still, they will contain pesticide residues and will probably have been exposed to excessively high temperatures to make them quicker cooking, which robs them of nutrients.

The "health food" version of rolled oats is usually called flaked or crushed oats and the temperatures these products are exposed to are supposed to be low and carefully controlled to

OAT
life-size

preserve food value. However, these flaked oats require longer cooking—allow about ½ hour.

With steel-cut oats you can hardly go wrong, for here the whole grain is merely sliced, and otherwise untampered with. The finer the slicing of steel-cut oats, the quicker the cooking—it varies from 20 to 40 minutes depending on the degree of coarseness. Whole oats in pristine state (oat groats) take 1 to 2 hours to cook. Whole oats can also be sprouted (see *Sprouts*), resulting in enormous increase in vitamin content, particularly vitamin B_2. Oat gruel (made by cooking and cooking and cooking whole oats until they become thick like a beverage) is said to be extremely healthful and was a popular drink in seventeenth-century London coffeehouses. Steel-cut and whole oats are slightly more difficult to digest than rolled, flaked, or crushed oats. All oat cereals encourage circulation and peristalsis and can act as a mild laxative.

Leftover oatmeal need not be thrown to the birds. While it is still warm, mix in some raisins and hulled sunflower seeds, press into a buttered loaf pan, and refrigerate. The loaf can then be sliced any time, and the slices sautéed in butter—delicious with bacon and eggs. Or add leftover oatmeal to bread recipes; 1 cup oatmeal will replace about ⅔ cup wheat flour.

OATMEAL PANCAKES

1 c. oat flakes (or rolled oats)	½ tsp. salt
2 c. whole milk	2 tbsp. honey
1½ c. whole wheat flour	2 eggs, beaten
1 tsp. baking powder	¼ c. melted butter

Soak oat flakes in milk overnight (if you give in and use commercial rolled oats, soaking is unnecessary). In the morning, mix flour, baking powder, salt, and honey into oat-milk mixture. Add beaten eggs and melted butter. On a lightly greased griddle, at medium-high heat, spoon small pancakes, cooking on first side until bubbly and then turning; try to turn each pancake only once. Makes about twenty 4-inch pancakes. Serve with butter and honey or maple syrup.

For other oatmeal recipes, see *Cereal*.

OATS, FLAKED Flaked or crushed oats are similar to rolled oats, but are usually not exposed to such high temperature. They therefore retain most of their original nutritional value, but take longer to cook than commercial rolled oats. See *Oatmeal*.

OATS, ROLLED These are oat kernels that have been hulled and flattened on steel rollers. They are often exposed to high heat which lessens nutritional value and makes them quicker to cook. See *Oatmeal*.

OATS, STEEL-CUT Steel-cut oats are available in coarse or fine grinds. They are often known as Scottish oats, for in this form the Scots, who are centuries-old experts in the eating of oats, appreciate them most. See *Oatmeal*.

OIL, VEGETABLE Vegetable oils occupy an important position in nutrition; it therefore pays to obtain the best quality available, even if it be somewhat expensive. How to recognize the "best" is a little tricky, but with a few basic facts under your belt you can surmount the problem with ease.

First step: Try to avoid commercial big-name brands. These oils are all extracted by use of petroleum-base solvents and there is real danger of carcinogenic residues remaining in the oil. They are also exposed to excessively high heats and refining processes, which leave them odorless, tasteless, colorless—and unnaturally healthless. They are also permeated with preservatives. Stay away from them.

How do "health food" oils differ from the standard commercial brands? In all too many cases, they are treated in the same questionable manner, except that no preservatives are added—and you pay a hefty price for that small omission. What you should aim for is a pressed oil in crude or relatively unrefined state. Pressed oils are obtained by use of hydraulic or expeller presses. The oil is forced by pressure out of the nut or seed or grain rather than being extracted chemically by use of solvents. Crude or unrefined oils are exposed to various degrees of filtration rather than to refinement by means of caustic chemicals.

Cast a wary eye on labels. Question the term "cold pressed." All oil-giving substances (with the exception of olives and sesame seeds) must be exposed to a certain amount of heat before they will yield up their oil. Question the term "unrefined." A truly unrefined oil is dark in color, thick in substance, and pungent in taste—and does not appeal to all palates. Question the term "virgin" (as in olive oil). As an indication of quality it is absolutely meaningless, for there are no standards governing its usage.

All properly processed vegetable oils provide excellent sources of unsaturated essential fatty acids, vitamin E, and lecithin. The type of oil you choose to use depends on your own taste or intention. Peanut oil is good for frying, and Oriental cooking blossoms with it. Olive oil is unsurpassable for salads, and Italian dishes would lapse into lethargy without it. Corn, sunflower, and safflower oils are all highly unsaturated and good for general use. Then there are sesame, avocado, walnut . . . Experiment!

Always refrigerate vegetable oil after opening so that it will not become rancid. It will keep longer if it is in a dark container, for the oil deteriorates more rapidly when exposed to light. Vegetable oils can (and should) be successfully substituted for hydrogenated fats such as margarine, shortening, and lard in many many recipes. Here, for instance, is an easy-to-make pie crust prepared with pressed vegetable oil.

PIE CRUST

⅓ c. ice water
2 c. whole wheat pastry
    flour
1 tsp. salt

⅓ c. butter
⅓ c. vegetable oil (preferably pressed oil)

In a small bowl place an ice cube and about ⅓ cup water. Into a large bowl, sift flour and salt. Add cold butter, cut into small pieces. With fingers quickly mix with flour until butter and flour form pea-size lumps. Measure out ⅓ cup ice water and add ⅓ cup cold oil into same container. Pour all at once into dough and mix quickly with fingers, forming into a ball. Roll out immediately or refrigerate for later use. Makes enough pastry for one double-crust pie or two single crusts. *Note:* In order to have a flaky crust, the butter must not get too soft. Therefore work quickly; if at any point the butter seems to melt, refrigerate for a few minutes, then continue the recipe.

OLIVE OIL The gnarled olive tree has been the purveyor of health and wealth since times of great antiquity. The Mediterranean shores were its earliest home, and in Homeric times olive oil was the luxury only of the very wealthy, who used it mainly as an ointment after bathing. Later in Italy, every single part of the olive tree found its use: the olive itself, ripe or unripe, as delectable item of food; the oil as adjunct to cooking; the oil as fuel for lamps; the oil as applied to the skin; the leaves and bark as a tonic tea; the resinous olive "gum" as a medicinal and perfume. During the heyday of the Roman Empire a prescription for the pleasant life called for "wine within and olive oil without."

Olive culture has now spread to many parts of the earth, and California, China, and Australia have joined North Africa, Spain, France, Italy, and Greece as producers of olive oil. Italy remains, however, the high priestess of the olive, and little can equal the highest quality pure Italian olive oil. Olive oil varies tremendously in quality, depending on the type of olive used, the methods of refining, and whether it has been mixed with other cheaper oils. The term "virgin" is so widely and loosely applied that it no longer is any indication of quality; originally it meant that an oil was from the first pressing of the fruit, as opposed to the second or third pressings, whose oil is of inferior quality. Olive oil when unrefined has a greenish tinge and a very pungent flavor. It is preferred in certain areas to the refined oil, and certainly its healthful qualities are more intact—but you might have to cultivate a liking for the strong taste.

Olive oil oxidizes less rapidly than other oils; therefore it does not need to be refrigerated to prevent rancidity. It is somewhat more saturated than certain other vegetable oils, but many a centenarian Italian has attributed his long life to the virtues of olive oil—and we side with the centenarians over the saturationists, and cherish our pure olive oil!

Use olive oil in cooking as you would butter. For a truly gourmet flavor, use half olive oil and half butter when sautéeing or starting a sauce. Try sprinkling olive oil and lemon juice over hot vegetables, rather than the customary butter—it's delicious, it's healthy, and what is left over is all set to be used as a cold salad. Olive oil is incomparable in salad dressing. Here follows *the* way to dress a salad.

SALAD DRESSING

Have on your table:

a vial of pure olive oil *a large bowl, no more*
sea salt *than half filled with*
a vial of wine vinegar *freshly prepared salad*
a pepper grinder

Pour olive oil over the salad. (A quart of salad will take about 3 tablespoons oil, but this is variable; you want enough to coat all parts of the salad with a thin layer of oil, with none left in the bottom of the bowl.) Toss the oil into the salad until everything is well coated. Then put ½ to 1 teaspoon salt in a large spoon and fill spoon with vinegar (ratio of vinegar to oil should be about 1 to 3). Stir gently until the salt is dissolved in the vinegar, then sprinkle over the salad; add more vinegar if necessary. Grind pepper over salad. Toss well and serve. Salad should be served either before (health food style) or after (European style), never *with* the meal. With this method of preparing salad, the nutrients are sealed in by the oil so that the vinegar and salt cannot leach them out. The salad stays crisper, and salt, vinegar, and pepper are evenly distributed throughout rather than being deposited in clumps. Make a ritual of your salads!

OREGANO Oregano, known also as wild marjoram and Mexican sage, is a hardy herb of the mint family. Its pungent flavor is often found in Italian, Greek, Mexican, and Spanish dishes. Use it sparingly, fresh or dried, or its taste will over-dominate.

TOMATO-OREGANO SALAD

3 large cloves garlic
1 tsp. dried oregano
¾ tsp. salt
¼ tsp. freshly ground
   black pepper

3 tbsp. olive oil (preferably pressed oil)
1 tbsp. wine vinegar
2 c. sliced fresh tomatoes

In a bowl press garlic cloves flat with the back of a wooden spoon. Rub oregano between hands to release oils and let fall into bowl. Add salt, pepper, oil, and vinegar. Stir and let sit for an hour or so. About 20 minutes before serving, add tomatoes, stirring to coat with dressing. Refrigerate briefly.

Serves four as a side dish.

PANSY TEA See *Violet Leaf Tea.*

PAPAIN Papain, an enzyme extracted from the papaya fruit, is available in pill and powder form for use as a digestive aid. Papain has the ability to break down protein and is used commercially as a meat tenderizer. In tropical countries, natives obtain the same tenderizing effect by wrapping meat in papaya leaves or surrounding it with fresh slices of papaya fruit.

PAPAYA LEAF TEA Papaya leaves contain papain, an enzyme that breaks down protein. The tea is therefore helpful in cases of indigestion and stomach disorder. It is often combined with peppermint, which strengthens its stomachic properties and gives a delicious taste as well. Add 1 table-spoon dried papaya leaves to 2 cups boiling water and steep to desired strength.

PAPRIKA Paprika is made from finely ground sweet red peppers, rich in vitamin C. The many varieties of this spice range from very sweet to very hot. The paprika most commonly found in the United States is bright red and mild in flavor. True Hungarian paprika is of more muted color and biting taste (there are, however, dozens of varieties and degrees of potency); if you are unable to find this, an approximation can be achieved by adding a tiny pinch of cayenne pepper to the more tame domestic paprika.

Paprika is used as a cheerful garnish on pale foods such as stuffed baked potatoes, egg dishes, and cold salads. It is a delicious seasoning in many fish, chicken, and meat dishes, and of course is imperative for Hungarian goulash.

PARSLEY Put parsley in every dish you can think of. It is enormously healthful. It contains vitamins A and C in large quantity, along with chlorophyll, iron, and other minerals. Parsley's subtle taste complements almost every conceivable food. Use it fresh if possible. Flat-leaf or Italian parsley is more tender and tasty than the conventional curly-leaf type. Parsley is a difficult herb to dry properly; when not carefully treated it loses its color and its nutrients and becomes bitter in taste. Make sure your dried parsley is a healthy shade of green; that is an indication of good drying procedure.

Because of its high quantity of vitamin C, parsley is often used in pill form as a source of this nutrient, and the pills are particularly useful in the treatment of colds.

Parsley tea, made by steeping 1 teaspoon dried leaves in 2 cups boiling water for 15 minutes, is useful in the treatment of kidney diseases, gallstones, and rheumatism.

PEA, DRIED There are dried split green peas, dried yellow peas, and dried whole green peas—all rich in protein, sodium, potassium, magnesium, phosphorus, iron, and vitamin B. They provide the basic elements for extremely simple to make and satisfying soups. Whole peas are somewhat more time-consuming to deal with than split peas, for they have to be sieved to remove the tough outer husk that slips off while they simmer; they retain a higher food value, however, just because of this husky element. Split peas have been dehusked and split; dealing with them is simplicity itself, as you will see in the following recipe.

Organically grown peas are usually in short supply, and so health food stores often fill the gap with ordinary chemically raised peas. There is nothing wrong with this, for the dried pea is nutritious in any form. But make certain you are not paying high organic prices for peas of supermarket quality.

SPLIT PEA SOUP

2 c. split peas	*1 bay leaf*
2 qts. water	*Salt and pepper to taste*
2 smoked ham hocks	

Wash split peas well. Put in soup pot and cover with the water (use vegetable cooking water if you have it). Bring to a boil with the pot uncovered; skim off any foam that rises to surface. Turn heat low and add ham hocks and bay leaf. Cover and simmer for 2 to 3 hours, until peas have disintegrated and meat is so tender it falls off the bone. Stir well, add salt and pepper, and serve. Provides a sturdy meal for four.
Options: Use ham bone or salt pork instead of ham hocks; or leave out ham altogether and add sliced fresh vegetables as split peas begin to be tender.

PEACH, DRIED Dried peaches are high in vitamin C, potassium, and phosphorus and contain some vitamin B. When dried without sulphur and moisturizing treatment, they are tan and leather hard. Soaked and stewed with perhaps a little honey, they are delicious; put the stewed and sweetened peaches through a blender for a superb sauce to spoon over yogurt, cottage cheese, or ice cream.

PEANUT The peanut is not actually a "nut" at all, but a member of the pea family that grows in a most interesting manner. A rather low bushlike plant, it bears flowers that then become pods; the branches carrying the pods elongate, bend down, and push their pods into the ground; and when the plant dies the mature peanuts (or ground nuts, as they are often called) are dug up. Botanists are divided over whether the peanut came originally from Africa or South America. Now, however, it grows prolifically in almost all tropical countries;

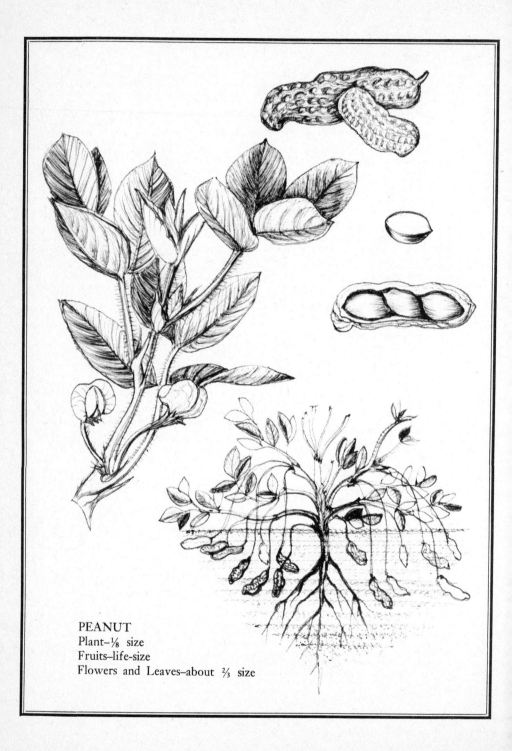

PEANUT
Plant–⅛ size
Fruits–life-size
Flowers and Leaves–about ⅔ size

India and China are large producers, as is the southern United States.

Peanuts are a very nutritious food. They are extremely high in protein and unsaturated oil. Because their protein is incomplete, however, they should not be relied on as a sole source of protein. They are rich in vitamins E and B, particularly in niacin. The thin brown skin of the peanut contains trace minerals and B vitamins. Its slightly bitter flavor is appreciated by some, denounced by others. Shelled peanuts are available with or without this skin, so take your pick. Peanuts lose nutrients when they are roasted—but gain delicious flavor. It is best to buy raw peanuts and roast them in your own kitchen, for then you can control the temperature, the quality of oil, and the amount of salt used. Many commercially available roasted peanuts are actually deep-fried at high temperatures in low-quality oil and oversalted as well. To roast peanuts properly: Place shelled nuts in a heavy frying pan over medium heat; stir until a roasted aroma arises; sprinkle on a few teaspoons of pressed oil, coating all nuts; stir in salt if desired.

Peanuts lend themselves to a wide variety of treatments— there is peanut oil, peanut meal, peanut butter, boiled peanuts, roasted peanuts. Peanuts can be used as nutritious snacks or as part of a meal. Sprinkle crushed peanuts on salads; use them as a curry condiment; add them to soybean and grain dishes.

PEANUT BUTTER The most popularly used "nut" butter in this country is that made from the peanut—usually the small variety known as the Spanish peanut. Because peanut-butter cravers run rampant hereabouts—and because many of them are children—it is important to realize the horrors that are perpetrated on this highly nutritious comestible by the food industry. Many commercially fabricated peanut butters contain as little as 75 percent peanuts. The rest is made up of hydrogenized fats (to prevent oil separation), sugar (for added sweetness and to mask the taste of inferior peanuts), emulsifiers (against oil separation), texturizers (to aid spreadability and counteract the butter's natural tendency to stick to the roof of the mouth), and degermed (for infinite shelf life) peanuts. Doesn't that sound appetizing!

Buy your peanut butter freshly ground and pure. Refrigerate during hot weather, and give it a stir before using, to redistribute the nutritious oils that rise to the top. Small trouble for the rich reward of delicious healthful peanut butter, as it once was and still should be. See also *Peanut*.

PEANUT BUTTER COOKIES

1 c. pressed vegetable oil	1 tsp. baking soda
1 c. peanut butter, un-homogenized	2 eggs
	1 tsp. vanilla
1 c. honey	2 c. whole wheat flour
1 tsp. salt	

Mix oil and peanut butter. Add honey, salt, and soda, stir well. Add eggs and vanilla, then flour. When well blended, spoon onto a lightly oiled cookie sheet by the teaspoonful. Press down with a floured fork if desired. Bake in a 350-degree oven for 10–11 minutes. Let cool on pan several minutes or cookies will crumble. Makes approximately 50 cookies.

PEANUT FLOUR See *Peanut Meal*.

PEANUT MEAL Peanut meal is made of finely ground peanuts. It is sometimes sold as peanut "flour." Like the peanut, it is rich in protein vitamin B_1, riboflavin, and niacin. It can be used to boost the nutritional level of baked goods—and to lend delicious taste as well. Try using ¼ cup peanut meal to ¾ cup wheat flour in bread and cookie recipes. Use also as a substitute for chopped peanuts. This meal is available roasted or unroasted; the roasted has a more distinctive nutty flavor.

PEANUT OIL The peanut yields a light bland oil that is good for salads and cooking. It lends itself particularly well to frying. Buy freshly pressed peanut oil, filtered rather than refined, without antioxidants, preservatives, and solvents.

PECAN This native North American nut is delicious and healthful. It is thin-shelled and easily cracked. Buy pecans in their shells whenever possible. Out of the shell they will only keep fresh under refrigeration (unless preservatives have been added). And avoid the garish red-dyed pecans that appear in the markets these days; the dye rubs off on the hands and goes thence to the mouth. Pecans are naturally a pleasing brown color.

The pecan has a higher percentage of unsaturated oil than most other nuts and is rich in minerals, protein, and vitamin B. Because of its high content of vitamin B_6, it has been used in the treatment of neuritis and arthritis. Remember that the pecan is a highly concentrated food, and eat with a measure of restraint (though it is often difficult!). Pecan meal is easily made by grinding these tender nuts in a blender and can be added to bread and cookie recipes for a nutty flavor and nutritional boost; pecan meal is also easy to digest.

PECAN CRUNCH PEAR PIE

Pastry for 9-inch pie
  crust
1 c. well-chopped pecans
6 c. sliced peeled pears
  (about 7 firm pears)

3 tbsp. mild honey
¾ c. whole wheat flour
⅓ c. "raw" or brown
  sugar
1 tsp. cinnamon
6 tbsp. butter

Prepare pastry and place in a 9-inch pie pan. Sprinkle ⅓ cup pecans over the dough and press in lightly. Chill the pastry while you prepare the filling and topping. In a large bowl combine the pear slices with honey and 2 tablespoons flour. Mix to coat all pears with honey and flour. In another bowl, combine the remaining flour and pecans with the sugar and cinnamon. Add butter cut into small pieces, and rub the mixture between your fingers until it forms pebble-size crumbs. Turn the pear mixture into the pastry shell and sprinkle the crumb mixture evenly over the top. Bake in a 375-degree oven until the pears are tender and the topping is browned—about 40 minutes. Serve warm or cool.

Serves six to eight.

PENNYROYAL American pennyroyal (as opposed to its cousin, European pennyroyal) is an herb belonging to the vast mint family. It makes a savorful tea, which is therapeutic as well—good for treating colds, constipation, headaches, sleep-lessness, and delayed menstruation. American Indian women drank pennyroyal tea as a birth control measure. The herb is most useful as an insect repellent; grow it by your door to repel mosquitoes, or by the doghouse to scare the fleas, or put the dried leaves in closets to ward off moths. Pennyroyal leaves rubbed on the skin will protect you from insects; the tea can be used in the same manner. Steep 1 tablespoon leaves in 2 cups boiling water; strain and serve.

PEPPER, BLACK   The peppercorn, long grown in trop-ical Asia, was the main instigator of the profitable spice trade that grew up between the East and Europe. In the Middle Ages Venice and Genoa waxed rich on its revenues; and even earlier, in the fifth century, the Visigoth king Alaric demanded 3,000 pounds of pepper as part of the ransom for Imperial Rome.

Peppercorns grow on vines in clusters of bright red berries. To produce black pepper, unripe berries are picked and sun-dried; the outer skin turns black and hard. Black pepper is widely used to flavor an enormous variety of dishes. It can be irritating to the stomach and intestines and is usually well avoided by those with ulcerous conditions. For those who can appreciate this pungent spice, *always* grind peppercorns fresh. There is really no excuse for using preground pepper; the dif-ference in taste is incomparable.

PEPPER, GREEN   This type of green pepper is not the familiar garden vegetable but the fruit of the *Piper nigrum* plant that yields black and white peppercorns. Green pepper is picked while unripe, and instead of being dried (which yields the hard black peppercorn) it is packed right away in vinegar. The resulting spice is green in color, soft in texture, and subtly pepperish in flavor.

PEPPER, RED   Red pepper is the fruit of an extremely varied group of plants known as the *Capsicums*. They are native to tropical America and the West Indies and range in taste from sweet and mild to pungent and fiery hot. They are rich in vita-

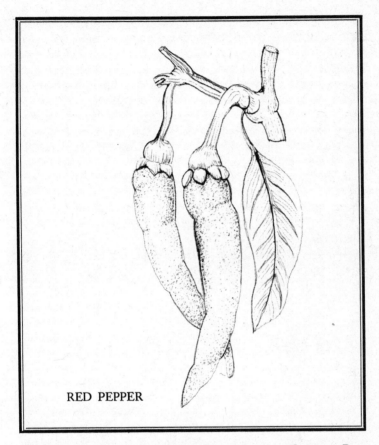

RED PEPPER

min C and have certain medicinal qualities (see *Cayenne Pepper*). Red pepper is prepared for cooking by grinding or chopping the dried pepper. Cayenne, paprika, and chili powder are familiar forms of this spice.

PEPPER, WHITE White pepper, like black pepper, is the fruit of the *Piper nigrum* vine that was originally native to India and is now widely grown throughout tropical Asia. White pepper is made from ripe bright red peppercorns, which are soaked to remove the outer coat, then dried, leaving a pale tan hard peppercorn. White pepper is slightly less biting than black and is used primarily to flavor light-colored sauces. Like black pepper, it should be freshly ground for superior results.

PEPPERMINT Peppermint leaves (fresh or dried) are used primarily for making tea. Its tantalizing flavor and healthful qualities make it excellent for young and old . . . and those of us in between. Brew 1 tablespoon leaves in 2 cups boiling water until desired strength is reached. Add honey and lemon if you like, and drink for pure enjoyment, or for relief from colds, headaches, indigestion, and nervousness. Peppermint tea is very soothing after an attack of vomiting and takes away the bad taste. Peppermint is rich in vitamins A and C. When buying bag "peppermint teas," be sure that the content is pure peppermint leaf as opposed to orange pekoe tea with the addition of a few peppermint leaves.

Oil extracted from the peppermint leaves has long been used as a flavoring in toothpastes and washes, chewing gum, and candy. Peppermint oil is a useful item to keep in the medicine cabinet, for it will alleviate toothache when applied to a bothersome tooth. It will also act as a mild anesthetic in cases of surface burns, and a dozen drops in a cup of herb tea may waylay attacks of diarrhea.

PIGNOLI (PIGNOLIA, PINOLO) NUT Except in rare Italian markets, this soft buttery nut is always sold preshelled. That is because its "shell" is a tough solid pine cone, full of sticky resin and dozens of tiny pignoli nuts, each encased in its own hard covering. It is a difficult and messy business to get the nuts out, and not a job that most of us would like to tackle. The high price of pignoli nuts is due to these extraction problems.

Pignoli nuts are imported from the Mediterranean regions. They are very high in protein (though like the peanut, this is not a complete protein), unsaturated fats, and minerals. Their delicate taste and soft texture make them suitable for use in a wide variety of dishes; add them to fish, vegetables, or spaghetti sauce. These nuts are used for cooking and not for snacking, and a few will carry you a long way.

Other varieties of edible pine nuts are found in Switzerland,

PIGNOLI NUT
life-size
Pine cone—⅔ size

Mexico, and the Himalayan regions. In the southwest United States and Mexico, the piñon tree produces nuts that are very similar to the pignoli (see *Piñon Nut*).

SPINACH WITH PIGNOLI AND RAISINS

1½–2 lb. fresh spinach	*2 tbsp. pignoli nuts*
2 tbsp. olive oil (prefer-ably pressed oil)	*2 tbsp. raisins*
	Salt and pepper

Wash spinach and cook it in the water clinging to its leaves, until just tender. While it is cooking, heat oil in a saucepan and add pignoli and raisins. Put the cooked spinach in a bowl and toss with warm olive oil-pignoli-raisin sauce and salt and pepper.   Serves four.

HERBED RABBIT WITH PIGNOLI

1 medium-size rabbit	*2 cloves garlic*
9 tbsp. olive oil (prefer-ably pressed oil)	*1 tsp. salt*
2 tbsp. butter	*¼ tsp. black pepper, freshly ground*
2 bay leaves	*¼ tsp. nutmeg, grated*
1 tsp. dry rosemary (or 2 tsp. fresh)	*⅔ c. dry white wine*
1 tsp. dry sage (or 2 tsp. fresh)	*2 tomatoes (peeled, seeded, chopped)*
	3 tbsp. pignoli nuts

The rabbit should be cut in pieces, washed, and well dried. Place oil, butter, bay leaves, rosemary, sage, and garlic (crush the cloves first with the back of a wooden spoon) in a pottery casserole or a Dutch oven. Sauté until the garlic just starts to brown. Put in rabbit, and brown it on both sides. Add salt, pepper, nutmeg, and wine. Simmer for 5 to 8 minutes, turning and stirring the rabbit until the wine has practically evaporated and the sauce is quite thick. Add tomatoes and pignoli and cover the pot. Simmer gently for about 20 minutes. Then remove the top, and continue to simmer while the sauce thickens—about 5 minutes. Serve on top of egg noodles or polenta.   Serves four.
Note: This recipe also works well with a 3-pound chicken, if there are no rabbits handy.

PINE NUT See *Pignoli Nut.*

PINEAPPLE, DRIED The flowers of this tropical plant produce hundreds of tiny fruits which coalesce to form the single pineapple. Rich in vitamin C, with some A and B and assorted minerals, pineapples also contain a digestive enzyme similar to that of the papaya. Therefore fresh pineapple, pineapple juice, and dried pineapple are all good for the digestion. Dried pineapple also makes a flavorsome snack.

PINON NUT The low-lying piñon tree grows in the southwestern United States and produces small pine cones that enclose the piñon nuts. These are very similar in taste and appearance to the pignoli nut of the Mediterranean, but they are far easier to extract from their cone. Piñons are not widely marketed, however, due mainly to the irregular productivity of the tree.

PINTO BEAN This tasty speckled bean thrives in the hot arid weather of the Southwest and Mexico. It is a good source of incomplete protein, amino acids, vitamin B, and minerals. The full flavor of pinto beans is best obtained by overnight soaking and long slow cooking—4 hours of simmering will do, but if you can leave them to bubble gently on the back of the stove all day, so much the better. Use 3 to 5 cups water to every cup of beans.

Pinto beans, which incidentally lose their spots with cooking, are used in soups, stews, cold salads, and the Mexican *frijoles refritos* (refried beans).

PISTACHIO NUT If you have never tasted an undyed pistachio nut, you have a treat awaiting: a plain tan pistachio with a green-skinned kernel, lightly roasted and salted—unsurpassable! These nuts are particularly high in iron, vitamin A, and protein, with sizable quantities of potassium, magnesium, phosphorus, and vitamin B. Pistachios grow on small trees that are native to Asia and the Middle East; they are now cultivated throughout the Mediterranean region and also in the southern United States. These nuts are most often found in Middle Eastern confections and in ice cream.

POMEGRANATE Those with patient spirits and time on their hands may enjoy eating fresh pomegranates. If you are not so inclined, pomegranate juice and syrup are available bottled in health food stores. Besides its tantalizing sweet-sour taste, the juice of the pomegranate is very useful in cleansing the bladder and kidneys. It also relieves constipation. Mohammed advised his followers to eat pomegranate, for it purged the system of hatred and envy.

The dried bark and skin of the pomegranate is extremely astringent and is an ancient remedy for tapeworm. It will also give relief from diarrhea.

The pomegranate is native to Persia and has been cultivated for many thousands of years. The fruit had religious significance in several Oriental cults and is often seen pictured on ancient Assyrian and Egyptian sculptures.

POPPY SEED The beautiful poppy flower owes its notoriety to the opium that is obtained from the flower pod. The seeds, however, contain no morphine, although a tea made from poppy seeds is said to have mildly calming properties. Poppy seeds can be either black or white; the black are of higher quality and white seeds are sometimes dyed to pass as black. They have a delicious nutty flavor and are widely used to flavor breads and pastries. Try adding a teaspoon of poppy seeds to melted butter and pour over cooked vegetables—lends intriguing flavor.

The poppy seed also yields a bland light-colored oil. It has been used in parts of Europe for salads and cooking, and as an adulterant of olive oil. It is also serves as a medium for oil painting.

POTATO FLOUR Potatoes did not enter the international cooking scene until the sixteenth century, when Spaniards in Peru came across Incas eating this all-American vegetable. The potato was enthusiastically adopted in Europe. By the nineteenth century the economy of Ireland had become so dependent on the potato that a failure of the potato crop brought the famine that started an enormous migration of Irish to North America.

Potato flour (also known as potato starch) is made of the entire cooked, dried, and ground potato. It is a very useful item to have in the kitchen. An ideal thickener for sauces, gravies, and soups, it cooks quickly and smoothly, leaving no raw taste (as wheat flour has a tendency to do). One teaspoon of potato flour will do the thickening work of 3 teaspoons of wheat flour. Potato flour can serve as a binder for ground meat and vegetable patties. It can also be used in bread-making to condition the dough and to give added nutrients (potato flour is rich in vitamin C, potassium, and iron); as much as one quarter of the wheat flour in any bread recipe can be replaced with an equal amount of potato flour. If you find yourself missing the mashed potatoes called for in a German loaf, mix 4 parts milk to 1 part potato flour and measure out this mixture instead of fresh potatoes—a not-so-poor second!

PROTEIN   Proteins are necessary to maintain all forms of life—plant, animal, and human. They are complex substances made up of amino acids (twenty-two are needed by the human body; eight of them essential) and are indispensable to the building, growth, and repair of human body cells. They play an immensely important role during pregnancy, lactation, and childhood; it is absolutely necessary to ingest adequate protein at these times. Inadequate amounts can result in permanent body and brain damage.

The American diet tends to emphasize meat as its prime source of protein. It is perhaps the easiest way to be sure of getting adequate protein, but there are many reasons to look for one's protein elsewhere—meat today is expensive and tainted with additives and pesticides, and from moral or nutritional points of view it is distasteful to some people.

But to eat vegetarian successfully requires a fund of nutritional knowledge. For it is not only the quantity of protein that is important but also the quality; many plants contain incomplete proteins that must be properly matched with just the right companion plant or the protein is of little use to the body. *Do not undertake vegetarianism lightly.*

Prime sources of protein are meat, fish, eggs, milk, cheese, soybeans, brewer's yeast, some nuts, and wheat germ. Beans and many seeds and nuts are high in incomplete protein. There are any number of powdered protein supplements on the health food market. They have their place, perhaps; but there seems no reason why with a modicum of knowledge and planning one cannot obtain adequate protein in a more pleasurable and interesting manner!

PRUNE Prune manufacturers are trying valiantly to rise above their constipation stigma. Cannot this fruit of the elegant plum tree stand on its own merits? For what is a prune but a dried plum—rich as it is in vitamin C, potassium, and protein. And delicious to boot.

Unsulphured, unmoisturized, unsugarcoated, unsprayed, sun-dried prunes are often so hard as to need soaking or stewing before savoring; be certain not to discard the juice—it is mineral-rich. Prunes are nutritious and good for the digestion; that they happen also to be efficacious in times of constipation seems superfluous to add.

PSYLLIUM SEED Psyllium seeds supply bulk and lubrication to the intestinal tract and are used in conditions of constipation. Psyllium seeds can be chewed, in the fashion of the ancient Greeks, or added to cereal or blended into vegetable drinks. One tablespoon of seeds taken twice daily should do the trick.

PUMPKIN SEED Pumpkin seeds (also known as pepitas) are crunchy and delicious, raw or roasted. Serve as a between-meal snack, or with cocktails, or toss them in with your fried rice. They are extremely rich in phosphorus, iron, and niacin and contain a good amount of protein, calcium, and other B vitamins. Renowned for their therapeutic effect on the prostate gland, pumpkin seeds are also said to destroy parasitic worms in the intestinal tract.

If you save the seeds from your next pumpkin, you can prepare them for eating: Dry them well for a few weeks, then peel off the tough outer skin. The inner kernel is edible either raw or roasted. This shelling process can be tedious; some pumpkins have seeds that are easier to handle than others.

ROASTED PUMPKIN SEEDS

1 c. raw pumpkin seeds   *1 tsp. salt*
½ tsp. vegetable oil

Put pumpkin seeds in a heavy frying pan over medium
heat. Stir in oil, coating all seeds lightly. Sprinkle in
salt. Stir continuously until seeds are puffed up (be
prepared for some to pop right out the pan!) and
browned—this takes only a few minutes. Incomparable
taste!

 RAISIN Raisins are dried grapes. They are mineral-rich
and a good between-meal food for children—particularly tasty
mixed with a few sunflower seeds. Try to obtain raisins from a
reputable health food source. Commercially "sun-dried" raisins
may be doused with insecticides and preserved with sorbic acid.
"Golden" raisins are usually bleached and the bleaching, distasteful in itself, destroys nutrients. Raisins are often moisturized
by added water (which you pay for) rather than by a careful
drying process.
    Use raisins in cereals, desserts, and bread. Or in this carrot
salad.

CARROT-RAISIN SALAD

¼ c. lemon juice   *¼ tsp. mustard*
½ c. raisins   *2 tbsp. mayonnaise*
1 tbsp. chopped parsley   *Salt and pepper*
2 c. grated carrots

Squeeze lemons and soak raisins in the juice. While the
raisins are soaking, chop the fresh parsley and grate
the carrots. As soon as the carrots are grated, mix in the
lemon juice and raisins to prevent discoloration. Add
mustard, mayonnaise, salt, and freshly ground pepper.
Serves two as a main luncheon dish, or four as a side
salad.

RASPBERRY LEAF TEA Pregnant women should
take careful note of this valuable herb tea. Raspberry leaf tea
taken from the onset of pregnancy until parturition is said to
help prevent miscarriages and to produce an easy labor and de-

livery. Use 1 teaspoon dried leaves per cup boiling water; steep for 15 minutes; take 1 to 2 cups daily. This is an old folk remedy that is still put to good use today.

Wild raspberry leaves are better than those of the cultivated varieties, but both are beneficial. If you gather your own leaves, make certain that they are completely dry before using; wilted berry leaves are said to be slightly poisonous. Raspberry leaf tea is also mildly laxative.

RED CLOVER TEA   The familiar pink-purple flower heads of the wild clover produce a tea that is high in iron, an excellent tonic, and a blood purifier. It has a delicate taste; add a few peppermint leaves for a hardier flavor. Red clover tea is an old and apparently proven remedy for certain cancerous conditions, taken internally, applied externally, or injected as a douche or enema—depending on where the cancer is located.

Red clover tea is also said to be quieting to the nerves. Gathering your own red clover sounds like a nerve-quieting activity, too! Dry the flowers in a dark airy spot and store in covered jars for winter use. To brew, steep 2 tablespoons blossoms in 3 cups boiling water for 10 to 15 minutes. Strain and serve with honey or lemon if desired.

RICE, BROWN   Rice is an Oriental grain that has been grown in India and China for over 4,000 years. Its cultivation was not taken up in Europe until the fifteenth century and in America until the late seventeenth century. So rice is a relative newcomer to the Western world.

Brown rice is the title given to rice that retains its healthful bran layer. Organically grown brown rice is not treated at any stage with insecticides, additives, or poisons. It is carefully milled, so that the bran layer and germ are unscratched, and this covering provides a natural preservative for the living grain beneath it.

Although brown rice is slightly lower in protein than various other grains such as wheat and millet, it is nevertheless highly nutritious and an excellent source of B vitamins. Macrobiotics consider it the most balanced and valuable of human foods. Its versatility in cooking can hardly be matched. An infinite variety of soups, stews, risottos, breads, and desserts can be built around a cupful of rice grains.

Brown rice is generally classified as short or long grain, and many regional variations exist within each group. Short-grain rice is considered to be slightly more healthful than long grain. All brown rice requires patient cooking—45 minutes to 1 hour. How much salt, how much water, how much time—all these are variable, depending on what *your* type of rice is, what kind of pot you use, even what the weather is like. Experiment, using the following recipe as your guide. Once you savor the flavor of brown rice you will never want white rice again!

BROWN RICE

2 c. water (for long-grain   *1 tsp. salt*
rice, try 2½ c.)   *1 c. brown rice*

Put salted water in a heavy covered pot and bring to a rolling boil. Meanwhile place rice in a sieve and hold under cold running water, stirring it with your fingers. Again with fingers, sprinkle rice slowly into the boiling water so that the boiling does not stop. When all rice has been added, lower heat to simmering. Put a well-fitting cover on the pot and simmer for 45 minutes to 1 hour.

If the rice is cooked too fast it will burn at the bottom; if cooked too slowly it will be soggy. Keep it at a slight bubbling simmer. The rice is ready when all the grains are tender but still separate; at this point the water should all be absorbed. If it is not, remove the cover of the pot, turn heat very low, and fluff with a fork until liquid is evaporated and absorbed.

Add butter, or tamari soy sauce, or chopped herbs. From here on it's up to you!   Serves two to three.

RICE, GLUTINOUS Known also as sweet rice, glutinous rice cooks to a rather sticky consistency and is used in the Orient for dessert dishes. It contains less starch than regular rice and is also available in flour form. Glutinous rice and flour can be found in Chinese markets and macrobiotic stores.

RICE, SWEET See *Rice, Glutinous.*

RICE, WHITE By white rice, we mean refined or polished rice. Rice whose vitamin-B-rich, beriberi-preventing bran
layer has been removed, along with the germ. Rice that has been
treated with preservatives because its naturally protective outer
coating is no longer around. Rice that has been fumigated
to give it long shelf life.

This processed rice is usually grown from seeds treated with
toxic substances to make them disease-resistant, with the "help"
of insecticide-sprayed ground, chemicals to control weeds and
water weevils, copper-sulphate to control algae, parathion to
control mosquitoes and larvae, and synthetic fertilizers. The
straw and stubble and husks are all burned (yielding air pollution) rather than used to refertilize the earth.

The result is a contaminated, nutritionally dead, starchy substance. But so white, so fluffy, so easy to prepare, that hordes of
Americans find it impossible to resist.

For a healthful tasty alternative, see *Rice, Brown.*

RICE, WILD Wild rice is the seed of a tall aquatic grass
native to North America; genetically it is not a rice at all. It is
delicious, expensive, and difficult to harvest. Indians in the
Midwest harvest and sell most of the wild rice that is commercially available. It grows in many other parts of the country as
well—often planted as a bird food by game hunters—but rarely
does anyone bother to harvest it. You may gather wild rice by
hand for your own use, but law says that *only* American Indians
may gather it for sale.

Wild rice has a much higher protein content than brown rice
and is also higher in iron and phosphorus. Delicious in any
setting, wild rice is a particularly fitting accompaniment for
game and is often used in stuffings. Wild rice can be mixed half
and half with regular rice, for a dish that is easier on the
pocketbook and yet exotically flavorsome.

RICE BRAN Rice bran is made from the outer husks of
the rice grain. We owe its existence to the fact that lots of
people eat white refined rice—which leaves a rich "waste" full
of vitamin B, calcium, phosphorus, and potassium. Use rice bran
as you would wheat germ: Sprinkle on cereal and yogurt; add
to baked goods.

RICE CREAM   This is a roasted brown rice flour that is used for making cereal or thick broth. You can make your own by toasting brown rice in a heavy frying pan, then grinding it to a powder in a blender, and reroasting it over medium heat. Store in a tightly covered container and use as needed. Ideal for thickening, too.

SESAME-RICE CREAM CEREAL

2 c. milk	½ c. rice cream
1 tsp. salt	2 tbsp. roasted sesame meal (or seeds)

Add salt to milk and bring to boiling point. Sprinkle in the rice cream, stirring to prevent lumping. Turn heat very low and cook covered for 5 to 10 minutes, until it thickens, stirring occasionally. Add the sesame seed meal. Serve with milk, butter, and honey. Serves four.

RICE FLOUR   The finely ground whole grain of rice yields a flour that can be mixed with broth to make soups, added to sauces as a clear thickener, and used in baking to lend a sweet moist atmosphere—very useful for those who suffer from wheat allergy. Rice flour is sometimes sold under the name of rice cream.

RICE FLOUR COFFEE CAKE

2 c. rice flour	1 tbsp. grated lemon rind
4 tsp. baking powder	(preferably from or-
½ tsp. salt	ganic undyed lemon)
4 tbsp. sugar (preferably	2 eggs, well beaten
"raw" sugar)	1 c. milk
½ c. raisins	2 tsp. vanilla extract

TOPPING

4 tbsp. butter	1½ tsp. cinnamon
4 tbsp. honey	1 egg

Sift flour, baking powder, and salt into a mixing bowl. Stir in sugar, raisins, and grated lemon rind. Beat together in another bowl the eggs, milk, and vanilla. Add to the dry mixture and stir until batter is smooth.

137

On the stove, melt butter and stir in honey and cinnamon. Remove from heat and beat in egg. Pour batter into buttered 8-inch-square shallow baking dish. Dribble topping all over the surface of the batter. Bake in 350-degree oven for 30 minutes. This is a light, moist cake, ideal for breakfast, afternoon tea, or dessert.

RICE GRITS Coarsely ground brown rice grains—or grits—are good for hot cereals and puddings, and wherever the fluffy texture of whole rice is not required. They are also quick to cook.

RICE POLISH The inner bran layers of the rice grain—known as the polish—are a by-product of rice refining. Rice polish is rich in vitamin B and minerals, but slightly less so than the bran that comes from the outer layers of the grain. Use as you would rice bran or wheat germ.

ROSE HIP The hip of the rose is the urn-shaped seed receptacle at the base of the blossom. When the flower is in bloom, the hip is green. After the petals fall, the hip begins to grow reddish. When it is bright red, the time for harvesting this powerhouse of vitamin C has arrived. The wild rose yields a hip that is richer in vitamin C than the cultivated rose. Rose hips can be used either fresh or dried (carefully dried hips should be a definite red color) to make tea, jam, syrup, and even soup. The hips do, however, lose a healthy percentage of their vitamin C in the drying.

To make rose hip tea, place 2 heaping teaspoons dried hips in a warmed teapot. Add 2 cups boiling water. Cover and steep for 20 minutes. Enjoy it plain; or add honey and lemon. Because of its high vitamin C content, it is excellent by the potful for the cold sufferer. Good for children, and in a bottle for infants. It is also said to be helpful to kidney and gallbladder functions. And its rose color is a joy to behold.

The rose hip is not the only part of the rose that is edible. Rose petals will add delicate flavor to everything from conserves and omelettes to cakes and candies. Rose water, which is distilled

ROSE HIPS–Tea Rose
approximately ⅔ size

from rose petals, is widely used in cooking in the Middle East. Rose water is also a cosmetic item, as is the essential oil of the petals. Attar of roses is the most sought after (and most expensive, at $100 an ounce) of essences, and it takes 4,000 pounds of handpicked *Rosa damascena* petals to yield but 1 pound of perfume essence.

ROSE HIP POWDER Powdered dried rose hips can be added to soups, breads, cookies, and candies. Blended together with ice water, honey, and lemon, rose hip powder will give you a refreshing summer drink. The powder is rich in vitamin C and has the gentle pleasant taste of rose hips.

ROSEMARY In its natural Mediterranean habitat, this savory shrublike herb grows to heights of 6 feet. Its small pointed leaves yield a flavor that no cook should ignore. Rosemary is a natural companion to lamb, and sprigs can be inserted through slits into a roast or used in a marinade for chops. All other meats and fish accept rosemary's flavor gladly, but use it with a sparing hand until you are familiar with its potency.

Medicinally rosemary has been appreciated for centuries as an antiseptic and was used as a strewing herb and to scent and disinfect sick rooms. Rosemary tea is useful for nervous conditions, headaches, and digestion and is an effective mouthwash. It stimulates growth of hair, applied externally as a rinse as well as taken internally as tea. Rosemary oil is also good for the hair; it combats dandruff and makes hair more manageable and easier to comb.

As you grind dried rosemary in your mortar or chop it fresh for Italian *focaccia*, you may recall (rosemary *is* for remembrance) that this herb is heavy with legends. It is said to have reached the height of Jesus Christ and at his death to have stopped growing upward and started spreading outward. The Virgin Mary purportedly threw her blue cloak over a rosemary bush, turning its white flowers to blue. The herb is said to stimulate brain activity and Greek students wore garlands of rosemary when going into examinations. It has long been a symbol of fidelity and in eighteenth-century England was carried in bouquets by brides and baked in wedding cakes. The smell of rosemary wood is said to preserve youth. The British claimed that the herb would not flourish unless the mistress became master of her household—sending wary husbands out in dark of night to uproot flourishing rosemary bushes!

FOCACCIA (ITALIAN FLAT BREAD)

1 tbsp. dried yeast
1 c. lukewarm water
1 tsp. honey
1 tsp. salt
2 tsp. dried rosemary (or
*   1½ tsp. chopped*
*   fresh rosemary)*

7 tbsp. olive oil (prefer-
*   ably pressed oil)*
1½ c. unbleached white
*   flour*
1½ c. whole wheat flour
1 tsp. coarse salt
*   (optional)*

Dissolve yeast in lukewarm water and let stand until it begins to foam (about 5 minutes). Add honey, salt, rosemary, and 1 tablespoon olive oil. Sift in half of the flour and stir well. On a floured board, knead in the remainder of the flour.

Pour 2 tablespoons oil into a 9 by 13-inch pan or a 13-inch diameter pizza pan. With floured fingers, press dough into pan in an even layer. Poke holes with finger at random, every 2 inches or so, in dough. Pour remaining 4 tablespoons oil over dough and spread evenly with fingers. Sprinkle lightly with coarse salt if desired. Bake in a 400-degree oven for 25 minutes or until well browned. Cut in rectangles or pie-shaped pieces and serve warm with soup. Delicious, too, warmed over for a second using.

ROYAL JELLY Royal jelly is a pale, creamy, sweet substance that is produced by the worker bees to feed the queen bee. The fact that a worker bee lives only a few months while the queen bee can live for three years has aroused much interest in royal jelly. Health food speculators have pounced on it as a miracle substance, a veritable fountain of youth, and there is no doubt that exaggerated claims have been made. However, analysis shows that royal jelly is extremely rich in B vitamins, particularly pantothenic acid (also well-supplied by brewer's yeast and liver), which is known to alleviate many of the diseases associated with aging—such as ulcers, graying hair, heart damage, etc. Royal jelly should be eaten fresh and kept refrigerated.

This expensive item is sometimes added to cosmetics, for which fantastic and rather dubious claims are often made.

RUE   This bitter herb was often used in medieval Europe to flavor salads and omelettes. Today it is still used as an herb tea to soothe headaches, nerves, menstrual pains, and infant colic. Brew 1 teaspoon dried leaves in 2 cups boiling water.

RYE FLAKES   Crushed rye grain makes a hardy breakfast cereal, a welcome variation on the usual oatmeal theme. Use 2 cups water or milk to ½ cup rye flakes and simmer for ½ hour. Serve lightly salted with butter and honey. See also *Rye Grain.*

RYE FLOUR   Rye flour is low in gluten, and it takes an experienced breadmaker to turn out a good loaf of pure rye bread. When rye flour is combined with wheat flour, however, it takes no special talent to concoct delicious and buoyant rye bread.

The finest rye flour is organically grown, and stone-ground from whole undegermed grain. See also *Rye Grain.*

PUMPERNICKEL BREAD

1 tbsp. dried yeast
1½ c. lukewarm water
1 tbsp. salt
½ c. molasses
2½ tsp. caraway seeds

2 tbsp. vegetable oil
2 c. rye flour (or meal)
4 c. unbleached white flour (or whole wheat flour)

Dissolve yeast in lukewarm water. When it foams, add salt, molasses, caraway seeds, oil, and rye flour. Stir very well. Add 2 cups wheat flour and stir in vigorously. Empty onto floured board, and knead in remainder of flour. In oiled bowl let rise in a warm spot until double in bulk. Knead down and shape into 2 round balls (or a number of small ones, if rolls are desired). Place on an

oiled baking sheet dusted with cornmeal and let rise
for 45 minutes. Bake in a 450-degree oven for 10
minutes, then lower heat to 350 degrees and continue
baking for 30 minutes or until hollow-sounding when
tapped. For rolls, bake for only 20 minutes after
lowering heat to 350 degrees. Makes 2 round loaves or
two dozen rolls.

RYE GRAIN Rye grain is grown in northern regions
where wheat cannot subsist. Its distinctive, somewhat sour taste
is found in north country cuisines—in Scandinavia, Germany,
and Russia.

Rye is rich in minerals and B vitamins, particularly in potassium and riboflavin. Rye grain can be used as a long-cooking
cereal, or it can be ground (if you have a small grain mill) to
make meal and flour. It is very useful to those who are allergic
to wheat.

A poisonous fungus known as ergot can sometimes infest rye.
Carefully grown organic rye is less likely to carry this parasite
than mass-produced commercial grain. Ergot contamination,
however, is rare nowadays.

RYE GRITS These cracked rye grains can be used for
cereal or as a main-course replacement for rice or potatoes.
They require slightly longer cooking than most other grain
grits—about 45 minutes. Use about 3 cups liquid to 1 cup rye
grits. See also *Rye Grain.*

RYE MEAL Coarsely ground rye meal will give the
crunchy texture that is characteristic of some types of bread.
Use it as you would rye flour. This unleavened rye-meal loaf
is ideal for canapes. See also *Rye Grain.*

ROGGEN BROT
(UNLEAVENED RYE BREAD)

1¾ c. boiling water	*4 tbsp. bran (or wheat*
1 tsp. salt	*germ)*
1 tbsp. honey	*½ cup wheat grits*
1 tbsp. pressed vegetable	*2 c. rye meal*
oil	

Mix together all ingredients in a large mixing bowl.
Cover with a plate or towel and let stand overnight. The
next day, press the mixture firmly into an oiled loaf
pan (or 2 smaller loaf pans). Cover pan *very tightly*
with aluminum foil. Place a pan of hot water in a 200-
degree oven. Put in bread and bake for 4 hours. Slice
very thin. Perfect for canapes and open-face sandwiches.
Keep *roggen brot* refrigerated, tightly wrapped in
aluminum foil.

SAFFLOWER OIL The safflower plant is known as
bastard saffron, and for centuries was used primarily as a scarlet
dye for silk and for cosmetic rouge. In its native habitat—India,
China, the East Indies—its seed was also pressed to yield an oil
that served locally for cooking and for lamp fuel.

Chemical analysis has shown that safflower oil is one of the
most unsaturated vegetable oils in existence, a fact that has made
it extremely popular in cholesterol-conscious North America.
Take care, however, to use safflower oil that has been refined as
little as possible. The refinement process employed by the large
commercial processors destroys the lecithin content of the oil,
without which safflower is of little use as a cholesterol reducer.

Safflower oil is light and bland, a good all-purpose oil for
kitchen use.

SAFFRON It takes the handpicked stigmas of 4,300 saffron flowers to make 1 ounce of saffron—which explains the
high price of this exotic spice. Saffron comes from a small
crocus (*Crocus sativus*) first cultivated many centuries ago in
Persia and Kashmir.

Saffron has long been valued as a dye and medicine, as well as
a culinary spice. The orange-yellow tones of its dyestuff have
held sacred positions in widespread areas of the world. There are
the saffron robes of the Buddhist monks; the saffron cloaks once
worn by Irish kings; the saffron shirts alloted to noblemen of
the Hebrides through the seventeenth century. In the time of
Henry VIII of England, ladies of the court took to dyeing their
hair with saffron; they soon found a less expensive method,
however—marigolds. The temptation to adulterate saffron has
always been strong. In the fifteenth century regular saffron

inspections were held in Nuremberg, and culprits were burned at the stake or buried alive—with their impure saffron.

Medicinally, tea made of saffron is a mild stimulant and antispasmodic. But its price is such that one would just as soon find a remedy elsewhere.

In realms culinary, Italian *risotto con fungi*, Spanish *arroz con Pollo*, and French *bouillabaisse* all demand the slightly bitter taste and flamboyant color of saffron. And the highest quality saffron is imported from these countries. Saffron is available powdered or whole, in thin dried threads. Whole saffron should be well crushed in a mortar before using. Remember that a pinch of this spice will carry you a long way.

FISH FILLETS IN SAFFRON-NUT SAUCE

COURT BOUILLON

5 c. water	1 medium-size onion,
1 small bay leaf	halved and stuck with
½ c. sliced carrots	4 cloves
	2–3 sprigs parsley

2 lb. fish fillets	¾ c. pecans
1 medium-size onion,	¼ tsp. saffron
chopped	1 tsp. salt
¾ c. fresh parsley,	⅛ tsp. black pepper,
chopped	freshly ground
2 cloves garlic, chopped	Juice from ½ lemon

Place all the ingredients for the court bouillon in a fish poacher or pot large enough to hold the fillets and simmer for 30 minutes. Add fish, adjust heat as low as possible (the fish should just barely simmer), cover tightly, and cook about 8 to 12 minutes or until the fish flakes when tested with a fork. Lift out fish very carefully so as not to break it and place it on a warm platter in a warm spot.

While the court bouillon is cooking, prepare onions, parsley, and garlic, and place in a blender along with the pecans, saffron, salt, and pepper. When the fish has been removed from the pot, strain 2 cups court bouillon into the blender, and blend for about 4 minutes, until the sauce is very smooth. Pour the sauce into a saucepan and heat but do not boil. If necessary, thicken with 2 tablespoons unbleached white flour. Add the lemon juice and pour the hot sauce over the fish.   Serves four.

SAGE How could a man die if he had sage in his garden, asked the ancients. This herb was once relied upon to cure all manner of ills—from colds to worms, from excessive sexual desire to sexual debility, from nerves to dandruff and gray hair. And surely there was some basis in fact for these claims, for sage comes directly from the Latin word *salvere*, to save. But sage's position in medical circles is not what it used to be, and no doubt we are the losers.

Sage has a pungent flavor that must be handled carefully in the kitchen. When sage is not properly dried it assumes a strong and undesirable musty flavor; try to use fresh sage or well-treated freshly dried sage. This herb is often added to boost the flavor of bland meats such as chicken and veal and is a standard ingredient in all types of stuffings. It has long served in the preparation of rich meats and fish, such as sausage, pork, duck, and cod, and sage is said not only to enhance their flavor but to make them more digestible as well. A cup of sage tea is also a pleasant way to aid digestion; pour boiling water over 2 teaspoons fresh chopped sage or 1 tablespoon dried sage and steep for 20 minutes; add honey and lemon.

VEAL "BIRDS"

1½ lb. veal scallopini
6 fresh sage leaves (or 2 tbsp. ground sage)
½ c. Parmesan cheese, grated
Freshly ground black pepper
½ c. unbleached white flour

½ tsp. salt
1½ tbsp. butter
1½ tbsp. vegetable oil (preferably pressed oil)
½ c. dry white wine (or dry vermouth)
Toothpicks

Have veal scallopini thinly sliced and pounded thinner. Cut into pieces approximately 2 by 3 inches. At end of each piece place ¼ of a fresh sage leaf or a pinch of

dried sage, a generous pinch of Parmesan cheese, and a few grains of freshly ground pepper. Roll up the veal and fasten with a toothpick. When this is finished you should have about 30 small "birds." Roll them in the salted flour. In a large frying pan melt the butter and oil over medium heat. Add the veal and sauté, turning to brown each side. This should take about 5 minutes. Then add the wine; stir gently with a wooden spoon until the wine evaporates a little and a slightly thick sauce begins to form. Cover the pan for 1 minute. Uncover and remove veal to a warm serving platter ringed with polenta or brown rice. Stir sauce, scraping scraps from the bottom of the pan and incorporating them into the sauce; add more wine if necessary. Spoon sauce over the veal. Serves four.

SAINT JOHN'S BREAD See *Carob Pod*.

SALT, SEA Sea salt is produced by the evaporation of sea water. It contains an abundance of trace minerals (iodine in particular) that make it superior to the pure chemical sodium chloride of land-mined salt. The sea salt most rich in minerals is gray in color; next in health value comes the carefully washed white sea salt for table use; third is the white sea salt that has been treated with additives to make it noncaking and free flowing.

Rock salt is found in land deposits where millions of years ago there were probably living sea waters. The passage of time has removed all trace minerals and left the pure chemical, sodium chloride, which many nutritional authorities consider detrimental to health. Commercially processed salt also contains a number of additives to make it more "manageable" that are undesirable in themselves—read labels with care. Detrimental or not, most people in this country use this chemical in abundance. Therefore, some nutritionists recommend purchasing iodized salt, particularly in goiter-prone areas. (Goiter is an iodine-deficiency disease.) A more natural way to supply oneself with iodine, however, is to eat fish, kelp, Swiss chard, turnip and mustard greens, summer squash, watermelon, cucumber, spinach, asparagus, and kale—all rich in iodine—and if you are a vegetable gardener, fertilize your plot with fish emulsion or seaweed.

Although we hear much talk nowadays of the harmful effects of salt, remember that salt is essential to human life and has been valued highly in times gone by—and still is today, in inland Africa and South America. To Homer, salt was "divine" and Plato labeled it a "substance dear to the gods." In many countries it has been valued as money. And we still speak of people being the salt of the earth, and of those who are not worth their salt.

Today, however, salt is often misused. It is widely employed commercially to disguise the taste of chemical preservatives and of inferior products. And in the kitchen it too often provides a cover for the blandness of improperly cooked food. Try eating a lightly steamed string bean and see how little salt—if any—it really needs. Salt is absolutely necessary to the life of man. But in these days when baby food, frozen vegetables, canned goods, baking soda and powder, prepared meats, soda pop, nuts, many snacks, and even drugs are loaded with chemical salt, one's concern should certainly be with getting too much, not too little. Use it sparingly, and when you do, use sea salt.

SARSAPARILLA TEA   Sarsaparilla tea is made from the dried root of a vine (*Smilax officinalis*) native to tropical America. It was introduced into Europe in the sixteenth century by returning Spaniards and began to be widely used as a cure for venereal and skin diseases. Recent chemical analyses have shown that sarsaparilla contains a number of valuable hormones that lend credence to the old tales of its power over waning virility, loss of hair, psoriasis, and syphilis.

In the Orient there is a root (*Smilax china*) with similar attributes, known to us as China root. American sarsaparilla (*Aralia nudicaulis*) is another of the substitutes for *Smilax sarsaparilla*.

SASSAFRAS TEA   This aromatic tea is made from the bark of the roots of the native American sassafras tree. The chopped whole smaller roots may be used, if you don't care for the bark-stripping exercise, but avoid thick pieces of larger

149

roots—they lack flavor. Boil the chopped bark or small roots until the liquid is a reddish-amber tint and a heady aroma wafts up, do not make it too strong or it will become bitter. The same bark can be reused several times before losing its potency.

Sassafras tea was used by the American Indians, who introduced it to the early colonists. It was prized as a blood purifying tonic and gave relief from all manner of ills—rheumatism, colic, bladder ailments, and such.

If summer flies bother your bowl of fresh fruit, place a few pieces of sassafras root in the bowl and the flies will vanish—so they say. Ground sassafras leaves are used in the filé powder that seasons and thickens the Creole gumbos of New Orleans.

SAVORY Savory is known as the bean herb, for it not only augments the flavor of dried beans but aids in their digestion and helps to prevent flatulence. Savory's slight peppery flavor, fresh or dried, is also excellent in salads, soups, sausage, fish, and poultry. Crush savory leaves on a bee sting to reduce swelling and pain. Chew the leaves for sweetened breath and brew them as tea for relief of indigestion and fever.

SEITAN Seitan is made from the pulp left over from the preparation of tamari soy sauce. It is dried in jerkylike strips that are high in protein and particularly good in soups.

SEMOLINA Semolina is a pale yellow meal made from the middlings of high-protein durum wheat. Widely used in Italian and Middle Eastern cookery, it is somewhat difficult to obtain in the United States. Some Italian markets and specialty stores carry it. Couscous, a North African semolina product, can be substituted in recipes calling for semolina, although the texture of the dish will not be as fine because of the more granular consistency of couscous.

SEMOLINA GNOCCHI

4 c. milk	1 c. semolina
½ tsp. salt	¾ c. Parmesan cheese,
¼ lb. butter	grated

Put milk in saucepan with salt and 2 teaspoons butter; bring to scalding point. Sprinkle in semolina very slowly, stirring with a wire whisk to prevent lumping. Cover and cook over *very* low heat for ½ hour. Stir in 1 tablespoon Parmesan cheese. Dampen a wooden board or cookie sheet and spread out the semolina in a ½-inch-thick rectangle. Square the edges and smooth the top with a spatula and cool for 15 minutes. Cut into squares about 1½ inches by 1½ inches.

Melt butter and pour ⅓ of it into a pan large enough to hold gnocchi spaced out so that they don't quite touch each other; individual oval ovenproof serving dishes work well for this also. Place gnocchi in pan. Sprinkle them with the Parmesan cheese and pour over the remainder of the melted butter. Bake in a 375-degree oven for 30 minutes until browned well and bubbling.   Serves four.

SENNA LEAF TEA Senna leaf tea acts as a mild laxative. Brew it with a little ginger added to counteract its griping tendencies.

SESAME SEED These tiny seeds are grown principally in East Asia and to some extent in Africa. African slaves first introduced the sesame seed to America, and in the Southern states it came to be known by its African name, benne. These seeds are extremely high in calcium, potassium, iron, phosphorus, and unsaturated oil and contain a good amount of protein. Always purchase the unhulled variety, for many of these nutrients reside in the hull. Organic, unhulled sesame seeds should not all be the same color—they range from very pale brown to tan—uniformity means they have been bleached or hulled.

Sesame seeds are usually toasted before using. This is easy: Place them in a heavy skillet over medium-high heat and stir until they are lightly browned. They are used whole or ground into meal (in a blender or with mortar and pestle) in cereal and rice dishes, as breading for meats and vegetables, in and on top of bread and cookies. Whole toasted sesame seeds are a welcome addition to French and Italian salad dressing. Ground

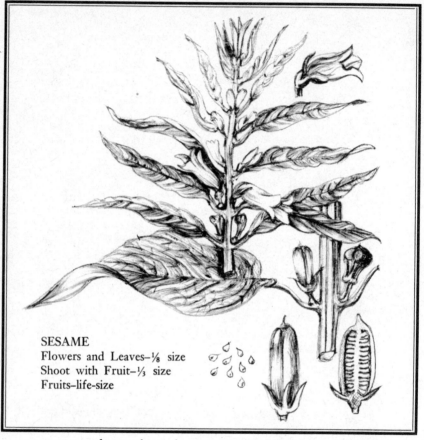

SESAME
Flowers and Leaves–⅛ size
Shoot with Fruit–⅓ size
Fruits–life-size

sesame seeds are the main constituent of that most delicious Middle Eastern confection, halvah. Raw unhulled sesame seeds can be grown into tasty sprouts.

SESAME SEED COOKIES

¾ c. butter
1 c. honey
½ c. sesame seeds
1 egg, beaten

1 tsp. vanilla extract
1 c. plus 3 tbsp. un-
   bleached white flour
¼ tsp. salt

Cream butter and honey well. Roast the sesame seeds lightly in a heavy skillet (see above). Add egg, sesame seeds, and vanilla to the creamed mixture. Add flour and salt and blend well. Spoon by the teaspoonful onto an oiled baking sheet, spacing the batter well for it tends to spread out. Bake in a preheated 350-degree oven for 4 to 5 minutes. Makes about 50 cookies.

BAKED CHICKEN WITH SESAME SEEDS

¾ c. toasted sesame seeds
¼ c. whole wheat flour
1 tsp. paprika
½ tsp. salt
½ tsp. pepper

1 3-lb. chicken, cut in pieces
2 tbsp. vegetable oil (preferably pressed oil)

Mix together dry ingredients. Dip chicken in vegetable oil and then into sesame mixture. Heat oven to 350 degrees. Place chicken, bone side up, in an oiled baking dish. Bake 15 minutes, then turn and bake 45 minutes more.   Serves four.

SESAME SEED OIL
The oil pressed from the sesame seed is light, mild, and healthfully unsaturated. It is fine for salads as well as cooking and is widely used in the Indian cuisine. Sesame oil is also used for making soaps, shampoos, and skin lotions.

SESAME SEED OIL, ROASTED
Roasted sesame seed oil is pressed from the roasted sesame seed. It is dark in color and has a rather strong flavor. It can be used for cooking and salads.

SESAME TAHINI
Made from creamed sesame seeds, this delicious spread is found in health food and Middle Eastern stores. It can be used alone as a sauce or spread, or mixed with miso, hummus, honey, peanut butter, or yogurt to make dips and sandwich fillings. See also *Sesame Seed*.

SESAME TAHINI

1 c. sesame seeds, raw
1 tbsp. wheat germ, raw or toasted

6 tbsp. sesame oil (preferably pressed oil)
⅛ tsp. salt

153

Grind sesame seeds and wheat germ to a powder in a blender. Place in a bowl and add the sesame oil and salt and mix well. It should have the consistency of peanut butter. Keep refrigerated in a covered jar.

SHAVE GRASS TEA The stems of a botanically ancient plant known as horsetail or pewter grass (it is said to be an efficient pewter cleanser) are used to make shave grass tea. It is a kidney and bladder remedy and aids in dissolving kidney stones.

Horsetail (*Equisetum*) plants in large quantities can cause poisoning of livestock.

SLIPPERY ELM The slippery elm tree (*Ulmus fulva*) is much smaller than the stately American elm. Its bark is used as a remedy for many complaints. The American Indians taught the early settlers how to chop the bark and brew it as a tea to relieve inflammation of the stomach and intestines, sore throats, diarrhea, and dysentery. The hot or cold tea may be applied as a poultice to soothe boils and burns. The bark can also be ground to a fine powder that is used to make throat lozenges to relieve coughs and sore throats.

SOLIDAGO TEA See *Goldenrod Tea.*

SORGHUM SYRUP Sorghum is a type of millet native to Africa and now also grown in the southern United States. Its stalks contain large amounts of levulose sugar (as found in certain fruits and in honey, as opposed to the dextrose sugar of sugarcane). Sorghum syrup is made from the juices pressed from the sorghum stalks. It is not as strong in flavor as molasses, or as high in minerals, but may be used interchangeably in recipes that call for it. This syrup makes a delicious topping for cereals, pancakes, and desserts.

SOY FLOUR Soy flour is a powerhouse of protein. It is very low in starch, inexpensive, and easy to use. No kitchen should be without it. A product of ground dried soybeans, this flour will boost the nutritive content of a wide variety of foods without interfering with taste or texture. Add it by the tablespoon to hot cereals, soups, stews, sauces and gravies, meat patties and loafs, casseroles, pancakes, cookies, and cakes.

In bread baking, soy flour can replace ⅕ of the wheat flour. It not only adds protein, lecithin, and vitamins E and B to the bread but also gives a smoother texture and richer crust. And the lecithin acts as a natural preservative—bread made partly with soy flour stays moist and fresh at least twice as long as plain wheat bread. The well-known Cornell protein loaf relies on soy flour for much of its nutritive content. This legume flour lacks gluten, however, and must always be used in conjunction with wheat flour when making bread.

Soy flour is available toasted or raw. The toasted flour is yellow and adds good color and a slight nutty flavor to foods. The raw flour is bland in taste, white in color, and often used for making tofu or soy curd. Lo-fat soy flour has had 99 percent of the oil removed. It is a high protein product, useful to those who are dieting. But remember that the "fat" in soy flour consists of valuable vitamin E and lecithin; and because it lacks lecithin, lo-fat soy flour does not have any preservative qualities.

ITALIAN-STYLE BREAD

1 tbsp. dry yeast (or 2 oz. compressed)	1 tbsp. salt
	2 c. whole wheat flour
2 tbsp. honey	1½ c. soy flour
2½ c. warm water	3 c. unbleached white
2 tbsp. pressed oil	flour

Mix yeast and honey into the warm water and let stand until yeast begins to foam. Add oil and salt. Sift in about 4 cups of the mixed flours, and stir very well (the more you stir the lighter the bread will be). Empty onto a floured kneading board, and knead in the remainder of the flour, adding more unbleached white flour if necessary. Let the dough rise in a lightly oiled bowl, covered with a towel and set in a warm spot, until it is double in bulk—about 1 hour.

Put the dough on the floured board again and knead

out all the air bubbles. Shape the dough into 1 very large Italian loaf or 2 smaller ones. Place the loaf or loaves on a baking sheet sprinkled with cornmeal, and let rise for another 45 minutes. Halfway through this last rising, make several ½-inch-deep diagonal slits along the top of the loaf. Bake at 350 degrees for about 50 minutes or until the loaf is brown and crusty and sounds hollow when tapped with a finger.

This recipe yields 1 enormous or 2 regular-size Italian loaves that are certain to please the most refined tastes.

SOY GRITS Lightly roasted soybeans are coarsely cracked to make soy grits. The grits are used primarily as a meat substitute or a food extender. Prepare them by adding 2 cups boiling water to 1 cup soy grits. When the water is absorbed the grits can be mixed into meat loaves, hamburgers, egg dishes, stuffings, and cereals. The grits are bland and do not alter the taste of the food to which they are added. Soaked soy grits can be refrigerated in a covered jar and used as needed.

SOY MILK POWDER Soy milk powder is finely milled soy flour. It is an excellent milk substitute for infants who are allergic to cow's milk. It is highly nutritious and may also be used in cooking, in the same manner as dairy milk.

SOY OIL Crude pressed soy oil is pressed from the soybean and is filtered but unrefined. Dark in color, it has a nutlike flavor and is high in unsaturated fats. It is excellent for use in baking, and the high lecithin content gives preservative qualities to breads, cakes, and cookies. Soy oil cannot, however, be used for sautéing or frying because of its tendency to foam.

Much soy oil is not pressed and crude. It is extracted by chemical solvents, refined, bleached, deodorized, and preserved. Avoid it.

SOY SAUCE Soy sauce, also known as tamari, is an extract of the soybean. It is made from soybeans (usually together with wheat or barley, sea salt, and pure water) that are fer-

SOYBEAN
Branch and Pods–
approximately ⅔
size
Seeds–life-size

mented for at least 18 months. Unfortunately most soy sauces do not undergo such time-consuming preparation. Many are not aged long enough, and monosodium glutamate is added to perk up inferior flavor; preservatives are also used. True tamari soy sauce has no need of additives or preservatives; if it develops a spot of mold on top, just skim it off—the tamari will taste as good as ever and does not need refrigeration.

Use a dash of soy sauce in soups or with vegetables, cooked grains, and meats. Its savory flavor will lend distinctive taste to your dinner fare. Remember, however, that soy sauce is quite salty in itself, and adjust the salt in your recipes accordingly.

CHINESE BEEF WITH VEGETABLES

1 lb. flank steak

¼ *lb. snowpeas*	*2 large tomatoes, peeled,*
2 *c. chinese cabbage,*	*seeded, chopped*
coarsely chopped	*2 green peppers, seeded*
½ *c. soybean (or mung)* **OR**	*and chopped*
sprouts	*2 medium zucchini, thin-*
¼ *c. fresh ginger, peeled*	*ly sliced*
and thinly sliced	

½ *tsp. honey*	*2 tbsp. soy sauce*
¾ *c. broth or water*	*1 tbsp. arrowroot*
1 clove garlic, chopped	*Salt and pepper*
1 large onion, sliced	*1 tbsp. sliced dry ginger*
6 tbsp. peanut oil	

This dish cooks very quickly. Therefore be certain to
have the ingredients prepared before you start to cook.
Slice the flank steak very thinly (this is sometimes easier
if the meat is partially frozen). Chop or slice all the
vegetables you choose to use, leaving snowpeas and
mung sprouts whole. In a small bowl mix the honey,
broth, soy sauce, and arrowroot. Place all the prepared
ingredients near the stove.
Put 3 tablespoons oil in a wok or large frying pan, and
heat until quite hot, but not smoking. Put half of the
meat in pan. Toss it around with a wooden spoon for
1 minute, browning both sides. Place on a warm platter.
Cook remainder of the meat in the same manner.
Place it on the warm platter. Add 3 tablespoons oil to
the pan along with the garlic, onion, and ginger. Toss a
few seconds, then add the rest of the vegetables. Stir
and cook for 3 to 4 minutes—they should retain their
crispness. Remove vegetables to the warm platter. Pour
the soy sauce mixture into the pan, and stir until
slightly thickened. Pour the sauce over the meat and
vegetables. Sprinkle with salt and ground pepper and
serve immediately.   Sumptuous eating for four.

SOYBEAN The soybean has been the mainstay of Oriental cuisine for thousands of years. The Western world has long been ignorant of the taste and nutritional delights offered by this versatile little bean. Extremely rich in high-quality protein, calcium, and B vitamins, this is the only legume that contains all of the essential amino acids; thus it ranks with meat, fowl, and fish as a prime protein source. One-half cup cooked soybeans is roughly equivalent to ¼-pound meat in grams of protein contained.

The soybean can be used fresh or dried, as milk or cheese (tofu), as flour or grits, as oil or sauce, and as sprouts or roasted snacks. The soybean is low in starch, easy to digest, and mild in flavor. It blossoms under a sprinkling of herbs and lends itself to an infinite variety of culinary treatments.

SOYBEAN SALAD

Wash 2 cups dried soybeans, cover with 1½ quarts water, and soak overnight. If the weather is warm, soak soybeans in refrigerator to avoid fermentation. The following morning, put the soybeans and their soaking water in a soup pot, add more water to cover if necessary, add 1 teaspoon salt, bring to boil, skim off foam, then simmer for 2 hours or until tender. Drain and cool the soybeans. Save the cooking water for soups, rice, etc.

Mix together:

soybeans, cooked and cooled
½ c. chopped celery
1 medium-size onion, chopped
½ c. chopped fresh parsley

½ tsp. ground black pepper
½ tsp. salt
¼ tsp. dill weed
½ c. mayonnaise (home-made preferred)

Chill well. Serve as a main course on lettuce, garnished with tomatoes, olives, and cucumber slices, for four to six. Or put alone in a bowl and use as a side dish.

SOYBEAN, ROASTED Roasted soybeans have recently been "discovered" as a snack food. They are tasty, contain more protein, and are less fattening than their roasted-nut counterparts. However, when buying them prepackaged, examine the label carefully to see that no preservatives have been added. Unfortunately the label will not tell you when the soybeans have been fried in cheap rancid oil. Really, it's best to roast your own. Here's how.

ROASTED SOYBEANS

1 c. dried soybeans	*1 tsp. salt*
3 c. water	

Overnight soak soybeans in water. Refrigerate while soaking if the weather is hot. Add salt and simmer for 1 hour. Drain, keeping leftover water for soup stock, and spread the soybeans shallowly in a baking pan. Roast in a 375-degree oven for 45 minutes, stirring every 15 minutes or so. The soybeans are done when they are lightly browned. Sprinkle with salt while still warm. Serve, or store in a well covered jar.

SPEARMINT Spearmint is the mint most often used in cooking—in the ever-familiar lamb sauce and the Southern mint julep. Spearmint lends itself to a wide variety of dishes: Mint-flavored butter adds definite flair to cooked vegetables such as carrots, new potatoes, and beets; and salads take on a Middle Eastern air with the addition of a handful of finely chopped mint. See also *Mint*.

SPICES Today we take spices quite for granted. But only a few centuries ago these same spices were the gold of the Eastern tropics; Europeans intrigued, fought, and died to obtain them. They were valued not only as seasonings but also as preservatives—an invaluable asset in days when refrigeration was far away.

Spices come from the root, bark, stems, leaves, buds, fruit, or seeds of trees and plants, many of which are native to the tropics. They contain strongly aromatic oils that are fascinating to cook with. Some people maintain, however, that these aromatic oils are an irritant to the kidneys and intestines and should be studiously avoided. But to those who have no such doubts, spices in moderation lend excitement to a vast array of foods. Explore them, with a light hand and ready palate!

GARAM MASALA

⅓ c. whole cloves
¾ c. cumin seeds
6 3-in. lengths of cinnamon

¼ c. cardamom pods, dried
½ c. coriander seeds
½ c. black peppercorns

Spread all spices on a cookie sheet and roast in a 200-degree oven for 30 minutes, stirring from time to time. Remove from the oven and cool. Peel the cardamom seeds by pushing the pods with your thumb on a table. Then grind all spices in a blender, ½ cup at a time. Or follow Indian tradition and grind them in a mortar. This recipe will make about 1½ cups and should be stored in a tightly covered jar. It will keep for at least 6 months. Garam masala is used as spice in many true Indian dishes. Following are two recipes that call for garam masala.

INDIAN LAMB

4 medium-size onions, chopped
3 cloves garlic, chopped
3 tbsp. vegetable oil (preferably pressed oil)
1½ tbsp. garam masala

1 tbsp. fresh ginger root, chopped (or ½ tsp. dry)
1½ tsp. turmeric
1 tsp. salt
2 lb. boneless stewing lamb
2 c. yogurt

Sauté onion and garlic in oil. Add garam masala, ginger, turmeric, and salt, and cook for a few minutes. Add lamb and brown it. Add yogurt, cover, and simmer slowly for 1 hour or until the lamb is tender. If the sauce is not thick enough, cook it down by simmering the last 5 minutes without the top on.
This is a mild and pungent Indian dish. Serve it with brown rice to four.

BEEF KOFTA

1 lb. ground beef
1 medium-size onion,
  finely chopped
¼ tsp. coriander, pow-
  dered

1 tbsp. garam masala
1 clove garlic, finely
  chopped
½ tsp. salt

Mix all ingredients together, and shape into balls the size of small walnuts. Refrigerate while preparing the following:

2 medium-size onions,
  chopped
2 cloves garlic, chopped
6 tbsp. vegetable oil
  (preferably pressed
  oil)
2 tsp. chopped ginger
  root, fresh (or 1 tsp.
  powder)

2 tsp. turmeric
2 tsp. garam masala
1 tsp. salt
1½ tsp. cinnamon
½ tsp. clove powder
½ c. water
2 c. yogurt

Sauté onions and garlic in oil. Add ginger, turmeric, garam masala, salt, cinnamon, clove powder. Add water and mix well. Put in the meat balls, and sauté them for about 10 minutes. Add yogurt, and stir well. Serve over brown rice or bulgur to four.

SPROUTS Make a garden of your kitchen! Raise fresh organically grown greens all year round, even if you haven't an inch of earth to call your own, or any sunshine at all. Any seed can be sprouted—alfalfa, mung, soy, lentil, grain, fenugreek, pea, garbanzo, bean—and with the sprout comes a great burst of new energy. Sprouts contain nutrients that do not exist in the seed; they are marvelous sources of vitamins B and C, minerals, and protein.

Growing sprouts is very simple. First make certain to buy seeds that are fresh and untreated with fungicides. Alfalfa is one of the most satisfying seeds to sprout—tastewise, nutrition-wise, it's beautiful to look at, and a mere 3 tablespoons of the tiny seeds will give you 4 cups of sprouts within four days. There are many methods of sprouting. One of the simplest calls for a quart-size mason jar with a piece of cheesecloth or nylon mesh stretched over the top. Put 1 tablespoon alfalfa seeds in the jar, cover them with water, and soak overnight. In the morning pour out the water through the mesh covering, rinse the seeds, drain, and set the jar on its side in a dark spot. Two or three times a day, rinse the seeds, drain, and set the jar back on its side in the dark. Within 3 to 4 days the alfalfa sprouts will be about an inch long and will completely fill the quart jar. They are ready for eating. Some people recommend exposing the sprouts to sunlight at this point for a day, to develop chlorophyll content. Store the finished sprouts in a plastic bag in the refrigerator, and start a new batch in the mason jar. All seeds can be sprouted by following this simple method.

Use sprouts in salads, sandwiches, blended beverages. Sauté them briefly in pressed oil and season with tamari; or add them at the last minute to soup—keeping in mind that too much heat will destroy their nutritive value and dry them out as well.

CHICKEN SALAD WITH SPROUTS

*1 chicken, 3–4 lb., in
    parts*
*2 tsp. dry dill weed (or
    2 tbsp., fresh)*
4 peppercorns
1 bay leaf
*3 boiling potatoes,
    medium size*
3 hard-boiled eggs, sliced
*½ c. sour dill pickle,
    chopped*
*½ c. soybean sprouts (or
    other sprouts)*

1 tsp. salt
*⅛ tsp. black pepper,
    freshly ground*
¾ c. mayonnaise
¾ c. sour cream
1 tbsp. capers
1 tsp. dill weed
Garnish:
    lettuce
    tomatoes
    watercress

In a pot, place chicken parts, 1 teaspoon of the dill weed, peppercorns, bay leaf, and water to cover. Put a lid on the pot and bring to a boil. Lower temperature immediately and simmer for 10 to 15 minutes or until chicken is tender. Remove chicken from the pot and put in the potatoes; cover and cook them until tender— about 20 minutes.

Meanwhile, skin, bone, and coarsely chop the chicken into pieces about 1 inch by 2 inches; chill in the refrigerator. Remove tender potatoes from pot, slice, and refrigerate briefly. Mix together sliced eggs, dill pickles, bean sprouts, salt, pepper, chicken, and potatoes in a bowl. In another bowl, mix the mayonnaise, sour cream, capers, and 1 teaspoon dill weed. Stir half of this sauce into the chicken mixture. Spoon chicken salad onto a bed of lettuce, garnish with tomato wedges and sprigs of watercress, and pour remainder of sauce over the salad. Serve well chilled as a main course for four.

Note: Strain and reserve cooking water to use for soups and such.

STAR ANISE See *Anise Seed*.

STEAMER, FOOD A steamer is indispensable to the preparation of healthful and full-flavored vegetables. This utensil is a collapsible metal basket (the best type is made of stainless steel) that will fit in almost any size of pot. The vegetables (or fish, as well) are cooked in the steam of the small amount of water that boils beneath the basket—the pot, of course, must be kept tightly covered. Prepared in this manner, vegetables retain the flavor, texture, and vitamin content that is lost in the more customary and unfortunate boiling process. Save the steaming water and use it to make bulgur, rice, or soup more savory and nutritional.

SUGAR, "RAW" First, a little about sugar in general. Sugar is the refined offspring of the sugarcane or the sugar beet. One hundred years ago the annual per capita consumption of sugar in America was 10 pounds; today it is *100 pounds*. Most of this sneaks into the body very quietly, in processed foods that have sugar added to make them taste "better" (canned vegetables and fruits, peanut butter, dried fruit, fruit juices); and especially in the form of glucose or corn syrup, an utterly tasteless form of sugar that is used as a cheap filler and emulsifier in everything from cheese to catsup.

Refined sugar is an extremely detrimental food. It robs the

SUGAR BEET
approximately ⅔ to ¼ life-size

body of B vitamins and contributes to nervous conditions, tooth decay, pancreas misfunction, acne, diabetes, stomach ulcers—and body tonnage galore. It most certainly is *not* the harmless high-energy food that sugar manufacturers would have us believe.

And yet the sugarcane itself is regarded as a kind of wonder food. It is said that sugarcane field workers who frequently suck on the fresh cane are notably free from cavities and diseases. (We have as yet to hear of sugar-beet chewing.) Sugarcane contains almost all the nutrients and enzymes necessary to sustain human life; it is rich in vitamin B and minerals.

What happens to all this goodness? It certainly does not end up in the sugar bowl. It goes into the blackstrap molasses that once was dumped as a waste product and is now fortunately recognized as a valuable food. When the molasses is separated from the sugar juices, what is left is true *raw* sugar—sticky dark-colored crystals. This, if one wanted to use the best of sugars, would be the sugar to use. Unfortunately it is not available now in the United States; there are laws preventing the entry of unrefined sugar to these shores.

So the raw sugar is refined and refined and refined until we are left with pure white sucrose. Then to satisfy the health food fans, molasses is poured back over the white sugar—a little bit to give that raw-sugar look; slightly more for the brown-sugar look. It's a put-on! And yet, we buy it! While trying to keep our consumption of this product to the absolute minimum, when the occasion calls for a delicate pastry or sumptuous dessert, we are at least thankful for that little bit of molasses clinging to the sucrose crystals. "Raw" sugar is a step in the right direction, albeit a small one, away from refined sugar and toward more healthful sweeteners such as honey, date sugar, and molasses.

SUNFLOWER SEED The seed of the annual sunflower is too little appreciated in this country. The American Indians once made great use of the entire flower, using the seeds, stalks, and roots for food. In southern Russia the sunflower is widely cultivated for the valuable oil yielded by the seeds and for the seeds themselves. The hulled seeds offer a valuable source of vitamin B, protein, phosphorus, and potassium. Some claim that the seeds gain special energy from the flower's assiduous following of the sun from early morning to sundown.

Hulled sunflower seeds, either raw or lightly roasted, make a delicious snack for children or for a cocktail crowd. Many of the preroasted varieties of sunflower seeds sold in stores are overcooked (destroying nutrients) in low-quality oil, over-salted, and may have preservatives added. It is best to roast your own—a most speedy and simple process. Remember that the incomplete protein of sunflower seeds is complemented by that of peanuts. Try mixing the two for a snack that is a powerhouse of high-quality protein.

SUNFLOWER SEED-PEANUT ROAST

1 c. raw hulled sunflower seeds
¾ c. raw shelled peanuts
1 tsp. soy sauce (optional)

2 tsp. vegetable oil (preferably pressed oil)
1 tsp. salt
½ c. raisins or currents (optional)

Place a heavy skillet over medium-high temperature. Pour in sunflower seeds and peanuts. Stir until a roasted aroma rises and the seeds and nuts start to brown. Add soy sauce if desired. Sprinkle in the oil, stirring to coat everything evenly, then stir in salt. Pour into serving bowl, and add raisins or currants.

CHEWY SUNFLOWER SEED COOKIES

½ c. soft butter
½ c. honey
2 eggs, beaten
1 tsp. vanilla
1½ tsp. cinnamon
½ c. whole wheat flour, sifted with bran added back

½ tsp. salt
1½ c. rolled oats
½ c. raisins
½ c. raw hulled sunflower seeds
½ c. sesame seeds
½ c. shredded unsweetened coconut

Cream butter and honey. Add eggs and vanilla. Then add cinnamon, flour, and salt. When well mixed add oats, raisins, sunflower seeds, sesame seeds, coconut. Spoon onto lightly greased cookie sheet. Bake at 325

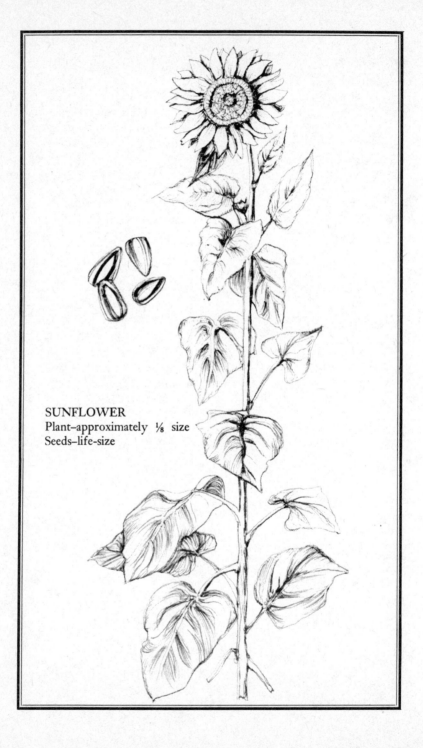

SUNFLOWER
Plant–approximately ⅛ size
Seeds–life-size

degrees for 12 to 14 minutes. Cool on rack. Makes 50 cookies. May be doubled.

SUNFLOWER SEED MEAL This meal is made from ground sunflower seeds. Prepare it in a blender (1 cup hulled seeds yields 1¼ cups meal) or purchase it preground in a health food store; keep it refrigerated. A delicious and healthful addition to soups, cereals, casseroles, breads, and cookies, it cooks quickly and has a mild nutty flavor. When making bread and cookies, ⅕ to ½ of the wheat flour may be replaced with an equal amount of sunflower seed meal. See also *Sunflower Seed*.

SUNFLOWER DROP BISCUITS

1½ c. whole wheat flour
½ tsp. salt
2 tsp. baking powder
½ c. sunflower seed meal

6 tbsp. vegetable oil
(preferably pressed oil)
2 eggs, lightly beaten
½ c. milk

Sift flour, salt, and baking powder into a mixing bowl. Add sunflower seed meal, oil, and lightly beaten eggs. Mix in the milk. Drop by the teaspoonful onto a lightly oiled baking sheet and bake in a preheated 400-degree oven for 12 minutes. Serve hot. Makes about two dozen biscuits.

SUNFLOWER SEED OIL The oil of the sunflower seed is an excellent source of unsaturated fatty acids. Unsaturated fats are essential to a healthful diet and help keep the blood cholesterol level in line. Be sure to buy pressed sunflower seed oil rather than additive-filled chemically extracted commercial oil. Sunflower seed oil is excellent for salad dressing and cooking.

TAMARI See *Soy Sauce*.

TANSY TEA The aromatic leaves of the bright yellow tansy flower (*Tanacetum vulgare*) can be used to make an herbal tea that will bring on delayed menstruation and calm hysteria. Tea made of tansy leaves and seeds is said to expel worms. In medieval times a dish of young leaves cooked with eggs was called a tansy. Tansy tea has a strong taste; in large doses it can be a violent irritant, so brew it mild and use with care.

TAPIOCA   Tapioca is a product of the roots of the cassava or manioc plant that is cultivated widely in Africa, South America, and tropical East Asia. Certain varieties of the roots are poisonous when eaten raw but are perfectly safe after cooking.

To make tapioca, the tubers are processed into small round white "pearls"—most commonly used in this country for the making of puddings. Tapioca consists almost entirely of easily digestible starch and is very low in minerals and protein. It is used mainly in the diets of invalids and young children, and aside from its easy digestibility has little to recommend itself.

TAPIOCA FLOUR   Tapioca flour is a farinaceous product of the tropical manioc or cassava root. This fine white flour is an easily digestible starch and is used for thickening broths and gravies. It is not widely available; arrowroot powder is used for the same purposes and is generally easier to obtain in the United States. See also *Tapioca*.

TARRAGON   Although tarragon is probably best known as an infusion for vinegar, please don't stop there! This heady and flavorsome herb does wonderful things to fish and is also used to advantage in salads, soups, sauces, and chicken dishes. Traditional French sauces such as béarnaise, hollandaise, and tartar depend on tarragon for their sophisticated flavor. In medieval Europe tarragon was also used as a breath sweetener and soporific.

Unlike most herbs, tarragon is not as pungent dried as fresh, for its essential oils disappear during drying. So use fresh tarragon *sparingly*, and dried tarragon liberally. French tarragon is of higher quality than Russian or "false" tarragon.

Try this delicious and unusual tarragon sauce the next time you serve fish or lamb.

TARRAGON SAUCE

1 lb. fresh spinach
1 c. mayonnaise
1 c. sour cream
2 tbsp. lemon juice
3 tbsp. dried tarragon (or
   1½ tbsp. fresh)

½ c. chopped parsley
  (optional)
½ tsp. salt
¼ tsp. freshly ground
  black pepper

Wash spinach and cook it in the water clinging to its
leaves until it is just wilted. Drain well and chop finely.
Mix together the other ingredients and stir in the
spinach. If you use a blender, just blend everything
together; the texture may lose some of the interest of the
hand-chopping, however. Chill and serve with fish
or lamb. Makes about 3 cups.

GREEN RICE SALAD

2 c. leftover cooked
   brown rice

¾ c. cooked green peas
¾ c. tarragon sauce (see
  above recipe)

Mix together all three ingredients, and serve chilled on
a bed of crisp lettuce or watercress. This is a delicious
summer salad.

TEA, HERB See individual herb teas.

TEA, ORIENTAL The topmost leaves of each branch
of the camellia-related tea plant are plucked for making the
finest Oriental tea. This plant flourishes throughout Asia and
most of the tropics. The many different varieties of Oriental tea
all come from the same plant; their differences depend on where
the plant is grown, how close to the top of the branch the
plucked leaves were, and how the leaves are processed after
picking. Black tea leaves are produced by drying, fermenting,
and roasting. Green tea leaves are dried and roasted without
fermentation. Tea has long been an honored beverage in the
Orient, where one legend has it that the Buddhist saint
Bodhidharma once fell asleep while meditating; he was so dis-
tressed at this that he cut off his eyelids, that he might never
sleep again. The eyelids fell to the ground, took root, and two

tea plants sprang up—whose leaves yielded a brew that could banish sleep.

Tea reached Europe in the seventeenth century and came to America soon after. It was at first regarded with moral and medical trepidation. One essay of the day protested that "men seem to have lost their stature, and women their beauty" due to overindulgence in tea. But the protesters fought a brief and losing battle, for Oriental tea was soon overwhelmingly embraced by the Western world.

Nowadays, however, tea is again under attack. Tea contains both tannic acid and caffeine, the same bugbears as coffee. And although 1 cup of tea contains less of these ingredients than coffee, it is still held by some to be an unhealthful stimulant and irritant to the body. Here is a method of brewing that is said to cut down on the tannic acid content of tea: Pour a little boiling water over the tea leaves; let it sit 1 minute; then pour it off, add fresh boiling water, and brew normally. Loose leaf tea is far preferable to the ubiquitous American tea bag. Its flavor is infinitely superior and it does not contain the dye that is found in some tea bags.

For those who feel that the drawbacks of Oriental tea outweigh delights, there are vast numbers of healthful herbal teas to sip and savor.

THYME   Legend has it that a soup of thyme and beer will cure shyness! Certainly thyme itself is anything but a shy herb. Wherever you plant it, it will spread rapidly; whatever food you add it to, it will tend to dominate. Keep a firm hand on thyme, or it will get the best of you. Its somewhat minty flavor adds good taste to poultry stuffings, salads, and steamed vegetables.

The leaves contain an oil known as thymol, which is antiseptic and used in cough medicines, mouthwashes, and salves. Tea brewed from the dry or fresh leaves has various medicinal effects that have been appreciated for many centuries. It has been used to treat whooping cough, asthma, and throat and lung problems. As a nervine it is said to prevent nightmares. It has been a prime ingredient in herbal pillows, which were once widely used to induce sleep.

CHICKEN LIVER PATE

4 medium-size onions, chopped
2 lb. chicken liver (organic if possible)
2 tbsp. vegetable oil

3 hard-boiled eggs, chopped
2 tbsp. cognac (optional)
¼ tsp. thyme, dried or fresh
Salt and pepper to taste

Sauté onion and chicken liver in vegetable oil until onion is tender and liver is browned. Put in a blender; add eggs, cognac, thyme, salt, and pepper. At medium speed, blend until smooth. If you do not have a blender, chop all ingredients as finely as possible and mash

173

together with a fork. Press firmly into a bowl and cover carefully with plastic wrap or a thin covering of melted butter. This will keep under refrigeration for about a week; the butter or plastic covering prevents discoloration. Makes about 1½ cups. Serve with rye crackers as an hors d'oeuvre or luncheon dish.

TOFU Tofu is also known as soy cheese and soybean curd. It is a staple food in the Orient, and each school of Chinese cookery has its own special way of preparing this delicate food. Tofu is very high in protein (some call it boneless meat) and in vitamin B. It is somewhat bland in flavor, but when well seasoned and combined with other foods it is a gourmet item. Use it in salads, soups, vegetarian dishes, and desserts. Tofu is somewhat similar to Italian mozzarella and can be used in much the same manner—you can even make pizza with it!

Tofu is made from soybeans or soy flour. Like any fresh cheese, it will keep for only a limited time—about two weeks under refrigeration. Store it covered with water in a bowl or jar. Tofu can be purchased in Oriental grocery stores—or try making your own with this simple recipe.

TOFU

1 c. raw soy flour　　　　　*4 tbsp. lemon juice*
4 c. water

Blend the soy flour with 2 cups water in a blender until smooth. (This can also be accomplished with a vigorous rotary beater.) Pour into a large pot or the top of a double boiler, and stir in the remainder of the water. The mixture should be completely smooth and homogeneous. Bring to a boil in the top of a large double boiler, or in a large pot over very low heat, using an asbestos pad or flame-tamer. Simmer for 10 minutes. (When the soy mixture reaches the boiling point it will suddenly foam up, so a big pot and a watchful eye are musts!)
Remove the pot from the heat. Add the lemon juice at once, stir, and let cool while the curd forms.
Place a piece of cheesecloth in a sieve or a pint-size berry box, and pour in the curd. Reserve the liquid that

passes through the cheesecloth for soup stock. Let the tofu drain until it is rather firm and jellylike in consistency. For a dryer curd, let it drain for a longer time. Store the tofu in a bowl of water in the refrigerator. Cut off slices as needed. Makes about 1 cup. Note: Toasted soy flour can also be used for tofu, but then the color of the curd will be yellow instead of the traditional white.

TOFU-VEGETABLE SOUP

4 c. soup stock (or water)	1½–2 c. sliced fresh vegetables, assorted
¾ c. tofu, diced in 1-in. cubes	2 tsp. miso
	1½ tbsp. chopped chives (or scallion tops)

Bring soup stock to a boil. Add tofu and vegetables and simmer for 10 minutes or until the vegetables are just tender and still a little crisp. Spoon out a little of the stock and mix it in a small bowl with the miso; add this to the soup, and do not let it boil again. Garnish with chopped chives or scallion tops and ladle out immediately. This quick and easy soup serves four.

TURMERIC This brilliant orange spice gives curry powder its characteristic golden color and adds a spicy flavor as well. Turmeric is a tuberous root of the ginger family and is native to India. The turmeric root is prepared by washing, peeling, drying, and powdering for use as a dyestuff or as a spice. Turmeric can be added to any curry dish or used alone to lend color and subtle spice to rice, cream sauce, and mayonnaise.

UMEBOSHI These are Japanese plums that have been salted and packed into wooden barrels where they age for three years. They can be boiled in water and used as tea, cold beverage, or salad dressing. The plums can be slivered and added to cooked vegetables, salads, and the center of rice balls. Umeboshi have a rare flavor that should be tried at least once!

VALERIAN TEA Valerian root is one of the strongest of herbal sedatives. It induces sleep and is an excellent tranquilizer. The smell of this tea is nowadays considered rather unpleasant; but in sixteenth-century England, valerian root was appreciated as a fragrance and was placed among clothes as a perfume. In brewing valerian tea, never boil the root directly; pour boiling water over the root and steep like leaf tea. Some consider valerian to be more effective when soaked in cold water for 12 to 24 hours, strained, and downed without heating.

However you brew it, do not take valerian tea for more than 14 days in a row. After a break of a week, another two-week stint can be embarked upon. In this manner, valerian's mildly addictive tendencies can be avoided, while you enjoy its calm benefits.

VANILLA BEAN The vanilla bean is the long seed pod of a tropical orchid (imagine an orchid that is more valued for its seed pod than its flower!). After harvesting, it is dried and fermented and then develops the characteristic vanilla scent while crystals of vanillin form on the outside of the bean. The highest quality vanilla beans are 8 to 12 inches long, black in color, with vanillin crystals on the outside. Either inch-long pieces, or the seeds scraped from the inside of the pod, can be used for flavoring. A large vanilla bean will give you a lot of use if kept in an airtight container; slice or scrape it out as needed.

Pure vanilla extract is hard to find. Most so-called "pure" extracts are made from synthetic vanillin, which is far cheaper than the real thing. As so little vanilla is called for to flavor any one recipe, it seems worthwhile to pay a little more for true and superbly flavored vanilla extract untainted by questionable additives.

VANILLA SUGAR

1 8-in. vanilla bean   *1 c. sugar (preferably "raw" sugar)*

Chop the vanilla bean. Add it to the sugar, and grind with mortar and pestle or in a blender. Place in a tightly closed jar for a week. Use measure for measure, whenever vanilla extract is called for.

VEGETABLE SALT Vegetable salt is not, as one might think, salt made purely from vegetables. Rather it is sea

VANILLA
Flower and Pods—⅔ scale

or earth salt that is flavored with various dehydrated vegetables. This makes a savory seasoning with a nutritional boost derived from the various vegetables.

VEGETABLES See *Fruits and Vegetables, Fresh Organic.*

VERBASCUM See *Mullein Blossom Tea.*

VINEGAR, APPLE CIDER True vinegar is difficult to come by these days. That is, vinegar that is alive, a little cloudy with sediment, with mother (a viscid clump of yeast cells that develop in vinegar as it undergoes the natural process of acetous fermentation) resting at the bottom of the bottle. Cherish the mother—it can be used to make another batch of vinegar.

Most of the vinegar available commercially has been deadened by pasteurization, which results in vastly curtailed mineral content. And a great deal of cheap vinegar is actually an imitation product fabricated from coal tar.

Living apple cider vinegar made from whole apples is not only delicious in salads and cooking but also possesses many healthful attributes. It is very high in potassium, a most important mineral. A couple of teaspoons of vinegar taken in a glass of water with each meal is said to promote weight loss, prevent hardening of the arteries, waylay mild food poisoning, and ease migraines, high blood pressure, and dizziness. Use a teaspoon of apple cider vinegar to a glass of water as a gargle for sore throats, then swallow a sip of the gargle. Apply apple cider vinegar externally to ease bee stings, insect bites, poison ivy, and burns. Use it as a hair rinse or in bath water to ease itchy skin. Add a touch of apple cider vinegar to meat marinades and broths; it draws the calcium out of the bones. Add it to the pickles you make; it helps them retain their natural food value.

The word "vinegar" comes from the French *vinaigre*, or sour wine. Good wine vinegar probably has many of the same healthful attributes as apple cider vinegar, but it is difficult to find unpasteurized wine vinegar in this country. You can make your own, however, by leaving a bottle of unpasteurized wine open and covered with a cloth for three to six months. Apple cider vinegar can be made in the same manner, using raw cider; the addition of a "mother" is not a requisite but hastens the acidifying process.

TROUT VINAIGRETTE

2 fresh trout (about 1 lb. each)
¼ c. raisins
¾ c. broth (or water)
4 tbsp. olive oil (preferably pressed oil)
⅓ c. chopped onion
1 clove garlic, chopped
¼ c. finely chopped celery
½ tsp. dried sage (or 2 chopped fresh sage leaves)

½ tsp. dried rosemary (or ¼ tsp. chopped fresh rosemary)
¼ c. apple cider (or wine) vinegar
1 tsp. grated lemon peel
1 tsp. salt
1 tbsp. unbleached white flour
1 tsp. soft butter

Wash raisins and soak in the broth. In a frying pan large enough to hold the 2 trout (scraped and gutted, but with heads, tails, and fins intact), warm the olive oil and sauté the chopped onion, garlic, celery, sage, and rosemary until onion is transparent. Place the fish directly on top of the sauté, and sprinkle it with the vinegar and lemon peel. Add raisins, broth, and salt. Cover the pan and simmer over low heat for 10 minutes or until the fish flakes when gently probed with a fork. With the help of a spatula, gently lift the 2 trout out onto a prewarmed platter; pull off the top skin of the fish, up to the head.
Blend the flour and soft butter with a fork. Stir it into the sauce, and let it simmer and thicken while you stir. Pour the sauce over the fish and serve. Provides joyous eating for two to four.

VIOLET LEAF TEA The leaves of the violet are rich in vitamins A and C. Their tea (also known as pansy tea or heartsease—it gives ease to the heart, old tales say) is an excellent tonic, which is said to soothe headaches and should certainly

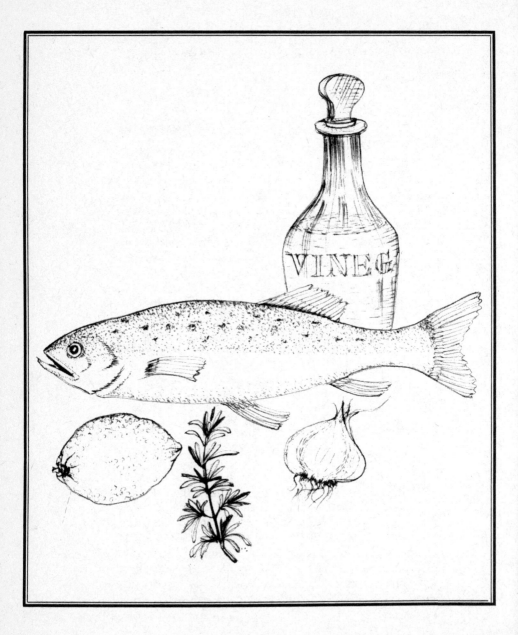

help to chase away a cold. Steep 1 teaspoonful of chopped leaves in 2 cups boiling water for 10 minutes. Fresh violet blossoms and leaves are healthful and tasty—try chewing a few on a spring day.

VITAMINS Vitamins are organic substances that occur naturally in food and are essential to human health. Vitamins first began to be isolated and identified chemically at the beginning of the twentieth century, and as years have passed, ours has become an increasingly vitamin-conscious society.

Attitudes toward vitamins are enormously various and often at odds. Many claim that as man has for thousands of years obtained all the vitamins he needs from his food, there is absolutely no reason why he should not continue to do so (even from standard refined supermarket fare), and that the business of vitamin supplements is so much hogwash. Others feel that if one is careful to eat only unrefined foods, whole grains, and organically raised produce, extra vitamins become necessary only in times of illness and special stress. Still others embrace a daily regimen of vitamin supplements on the grounds that our food is so denatured that it cannot possibly supply all the necessary nutrients—and that this is accentuated by a sedentary way of life that cuts down on the amount of food we need but not on the amount of vitamins our bodies require.

The debate over whether one should take synthetic or natural vitamins is also a large one. Many scientists assure us that because vitamins are in essence mere chemicals, they can be reproduced with exactitude in the laboratory. However, the make-up of a vitamin is not so simple. It can contain other nutritive elements and patterns that have not yet been isolated and that are essential to the proper absorption of the vitamin. Natural vitamins supply the needed nutrient in its natural food setting; such vitamins are therefore absorbed more completely and are also much less likely to produce the allergic reactions and toxic effects so common to synthetic vitamins. There are now many companies anxious to cash in on the natural vitamin trend, and not all are to be trusted. Natural vitamins should be concentrates of actual food substances, with no artificial coloring or flavoring added; examine labels and when in doubt rely on well-known time-proven brands. Ideally, all vitamins should be taken under the guidance of a doctor or trained nutritionist.

WAKAME   This seaweed is found in the cold turbulent waters of northern Japan and has a variety of uses. It may be added to soups or soaked for 15 minutes and then cooked by itself or with other vegetables. It can also be flapped over a burner flame until crisp, then crumbled and sprinkled over rice or noodles or served plain as a condiment. Wakame is rich in iodine and trace minerals.

WALNUT   There are many varieties of walnut trees that grow from China, through Europe, to North America. Their wood is usually highly valued for carpentry, and their leaves and nutshells for a black dye. Their kernels yield an oil used by both cooks and artists. The delicious kernels produced by most walnut trees are high in incomplete protein, unsaturated fatty acids, B vitamins, potassium, phosphorus, and trace minerals. Black walnuts, which are indigenous to North America, are tedious to shell but contain more nutrients than English walnuts. Two or three walnuts a day are said to alleviate bursitis symptoms.

Commercially treated walnuts are often bleached with lye to produce uniformity of color and are gassed to make shelling easier. Try to obtain these nuts in pristine state.

WALNUT OIL   This highly unsaturated oil is cold pressed from dried walnuts. Walnut oil has a definite nutty flavor and is not appreciated by everyone; so try it first in small amounts, in salads or cooking.

WATERMELON TEA   Crush watermelon seeds in a blender or mortar and steep 1 tablespoonful in 2 cups boiling water for ½ hour. Strain this brew and you will have a tea that is said to be helpful for kidney problems and high blood pressure.

WHEAT, CRACKED   The cracked grain of wheat—each kernel is split into about 4 or 5 pieces—has all the nutri-

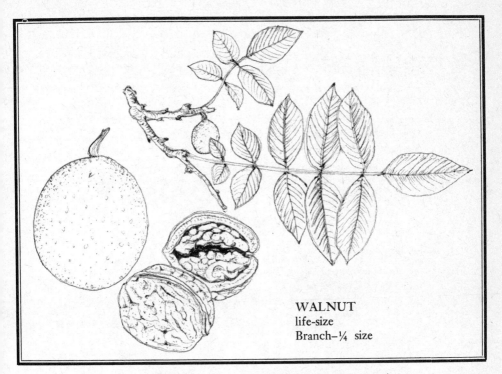

WALNUT
life-size
Branch–¼ size

tional values found in whole grain wheat, plus a convenience factor. It is short-cooking; as a cereal or a rice substitute, it can be whipped up in about 10 minutes, using 1 cup grain to 2 cups water or milk or broth. It can also be eaten without cooking, if soaked in water to cover overnight, making it a good item for camping trips. And it can be used as a binder in meat loaves and hamburgers, and in soups and stews. See also *Wheat Grain*.

WHEAT GERM, RAW   The germ is the embryo of the wheat kernel, its veritable life force. It is one of the richest known sources of vitamins E and B_1 and contains iron and protein. Unfortunately it is considered expendable—even undesirable—by large wheat processors, and its healthful presence is not to be found in the refined flour and cereals that crowd the supermarket shelves. The vitamin E-rich oil of the wheat germ soon becomes rancid unless refrigerated, so it has no place in the denatured flours that are meant to last forever in vast storage bins and on market shelves. The only advantage to this situation is that there is a lot of plain pure wheat germ to be had, and its healthful presence should be felt in every kitchen.

Raw wheat germ must be kept refrigerated, in a tightly covered container. It can be cooked in milk as a breakfast cereal or mixed with other cereals to strengthen their nutritional value. It can be added to bread dough but should be simmered in milk or lightly toasted first. If you like the taste of raw wheat germ, sprinkle it over yogurt and cottage cheese dishes. If toasted wheat germ is preferred, roast it lightly in a heavy skillet on top of the stove or bake it in the oven (see *Wheat Germ, Toasted*).

BAKED STUFFED ZUCCHINI

6 medium-large zucchini (8–10 in. long)
8 tbsp. olive oil (preferably pressed oil)
4 medium-size onions, chopped
3 cloves garlic, chopped
¼ c. fresh parsley, chopped (or 2 tbsp. dry)
½ tsp. fresh oregano, chopped (or ¼ tsp. dry)

½ tsp. fresh basil, chopped (or ¼ tsp. dry)
1½ tsp. salt
¼ tsp. black pepper, freshly ground
6 tbsp. Parmesan cheese, grated
¼ c. whole wheat bread crumbs (bread crumbs can be made in blender or crumbled finely by hand)

TOPPING

½ c. whole wheat bread crumbs
¼ c. wheat germ, raw or toasted
⅔ c. Parmesan cheese, grated

½ tsp. salt
⅛ tsp. black pepper, freshly ground
¼ tsp. paprika

Slice the zucchini in half lengthwise and scoop out the insides, leaving walls about ¼ inch thick. Place the zucchini shells in an oiled baking dish and bake at 300 degrees for ½ hour. Meanwhile, sauté in oil the onions, garlic, and coarsely chopped zucchini pulp until all are tender. Then add parsley, oregano, basil, salt, and pepper and simmer covered for 5 minutes. Remove from stove, mash with a fork, and add Parmesan cheese and bread crumbs. In a separate bowl mix together the topping ingredients.

Fill the baked zucchini shells with the pulp mixture and cover with topping. Bake at 300 degrees for 30 minutes.

Serves four to five.

Note: If there is not enough filling for all the zucchini shells, save the shells to put in soup.

WHEAT GERM, TOASTED Toasted wheat germ has a crisp nutlike flavor that many people savor by the spoonful alone. But it has a myriad of other uses as well. Use it as a cereal or on other cereal; use it along with or instead of bread crumbs for topping casseroles or breading meats and fish; add it to cookies and breads; use it in crumb toppings for desserts.

Wheat germ loses some of its health value when it is toasted, but the loss can be kept to a minimum if you toast it yourself or buy carefully prepared germ from a health food store. Commercially prepared toasted wheat germ (and this includes some health food brands) often has had its vitamin E rich oil removed. See also *Wheat Germ, Raw*.

TOASTED WHEAT GERM

2 c. raw wheat germ

Put the wheat germ in a heavy skillet over medium-high heat and roast, stirring, until a toasted aroma arises and the germ is lightly browned. Cool and store in a tightly covered container.

Or spread the raw wheat germ on a baking sheet and roast in a preheated 300-degree oven for 10 to 15 minutes or until lightly browned. Cool and store in a tightly covered container.

Toasted wheat germ does not require refrigeration unless the weather is particularly hot or you plan to keep it for over a month.

WHEAT GERM AND MIDDLINGS This highly nutritious quick-cooking cereal is made of raw wheat germ mixed with fine particles of bran. To prepare for breakfast, cook 1 cup wheat germ and middlings in 2 cups salted water or milk for about 15 minutes. Wheat germ and middlings can also be added to breads and cookies.

WHEAT GERM FLOUR Wheat germ flour is made by finely grinding raw wheat germ. It can be added to breads, cakes, and cookies, and lends a finer texture to baked goods than does the whole wheat germ. This highly nutritious item is very perishable and should be kept refrigerated.

WHEAT GRAIN Whole wheat grains are rich in magnesium, iron, phosphorus, vitamins B and E, carbohydrates, and numerous trace minerals. By the time the food industry has finished processing this nutritious grain for flours and cereals, there is little left but carbohydrates—and a few synthetic nutrients thrown in for good measure.

Whole grains of wheat can be used for cereal, but they take a *lot* of cooking. Usually wheat grain is purchased by those who grind their own flour. The taste and nutritional value of freshly ground flour are unsurpassable. So if you are really into making your own bread, consider investing in a small stone grinding mill (expensive) or a hand grinder (inexpensive). Wheat grain preserves itself with its own hard covering, so problems of refrigeration are eliminated.

WHEAT GRITS The whole wheat kernel is coarsely ground to obtain wheat grits. Grits are similar to cracked wheat but finer in grind. Add to bread, cereal, meat loaf, and hamburgers. See also *Wheat Grain*.

WHEY POWDER During the making of cheese, the milk separates into curds and whey. The whey is watery, somewhat tart, and very high in B vitamins. Whey is available in dried form and is a nutritious addition to blended beverages. Like other cultured milk products it fosters the growth of necessary bacteria in the intestinal tract and aids digestion. Whey powder can also be added to baked goods.

WHITE FLOUR, UNBLEACHED Unbleached white flour provides a halfway point where those who have turned their backs on refined foods can rest their senses before climbing on to more exclusive use of whole grains. This flour certainly is not the epitome of healthfulness, but it is a far sight better than the bleached white nonsense that is found in our supermarkets. It has had most of the bran and germ removed but has not been bleached with harmful chlorides and is often grown organically. It is very useful if your tastes lean toward flaky French pastries, light airy cakes, and Italian loaves of bread. It can be substituted in any recipe calling for white flour.

If you would like to gradually wean your family (and possibly yourself) away from lily-white bread, start by using unbleached white flour mixed with ordinary dead white flour; then move on to just unbleached white; then start adding whole wheat flour by the half cupful . . . Chances are the delicious taste of whole grains will creep up on everyone until it is accepted as the norm.

WHOLE WHEAT BREAD FLOUR Whole wheat flour is making a comeback. And it is about time. How tasteless and chemically manipulated white flour could have eclipsed the rare goodness of whole grain flour is somewhat mysterious; perhaps in the deluge of easily available cheap white flour, people simply forgot what *true* flour can actually do to a loaf of bread.

In making whole wheat flour, the entire kernel of wheat has traditionally been stone ground between enormous round buhr stones. The molecular structure of the wheat kernel remains intact and the flour does not reach high temperatures, thus ensuring the preservation of essential nutrients that are destroyed by commercial milling techniques. Recently another method of grinding—pneumatic milling—has laid claim to the same nutritional results as traditional stone grinding.

True whole wheat flour is not available in ordinary commercial stores. What is marketed as "whole wheat flour" is usually bleached flour with some bran added to give a whole grain "look." The germ, the most essential ingredient, is entirely missing because the germ possesses an oil that in time becomes rancid without refrigeration, and its presence is therefore not conducive to the endless shelf life required of commercial foodstuffs these days.

When buying whole wheat flour in a health food store, be careful to pick a brand that seems to have a high sales turnover. The longer flour sits on the shelf, the more nutrients it loses. And do not buy more than enough to last you a month; it is best to buy small quantities frequently, to ensure that the flour does not get stale on *your* shelf. Of course the ideal way to have whole grain flour is to grind it yourself, as you need it. Second best—find a mill or store that will grind it for you. The fresher the grind, the better the taste and the higher the nutritional value.

Whole wheat flour is an excellent source of B vitamins and also contains magnesium, potassium, iron, vitamin E, and protein. Most of these nutrients are concentrated in the bran and germ of the wheat. When they are removed by refining, no amount of "enrichment" with synthetic nutrients is going to restore the natural healthful state of the flour.

Whole wheat flour can be made from hard (spring) wheat or soft (winter wheat). Hard wheat contains more protein, in the form of gluten, and makes the best bread. Soft wheat is used for all-purpose and pastry flour, although it can be blended with hard wheat to make bread.

WHOLE WHEAT BREAD

1 tbsp. dry yeast (or 2 oz. compressed)
½ c. lukewarm water
3 tbsp. pressed oil (soy is good)
2 tbsp. honey or molasses
2 c. water or milk (lukewarm)
1½ tsp. salt
5½ c. whole wheat flour

Dissolve yeast in ½ cup lukewarm water. Add oil and honey and stir well. Add lukewarm water or milk; then sift in salt and half of the flour. Stir very well. Add more flour until the dough is too stiff to stir. Put it onto a floured board and knead in the remainder of the flour, using more flour if necessary, until the dough is no longer sticky and forms a smooth neat ball.

This should take 5 to 10 minutes of kneading.

Place the ball of dough in a large lightly oiled bowl, cover with a tea towel, and place in a warm spot—over a pilot light or on a slightly warm radiator. Let it rise until double in bulk (about 1 hour). Punch down the dough, kneading lightly to express all the air. Shape into 2 loaves and place in oiled bread pans.

Set the oven at 375 degrees. Let the loaves rise (again covered, in a warm spot) until dough just reaches the top of the pans. Put in the oven and bake for 10 minutes. Then turn the oven down to 350 degrees and continue baking for 40 minutes or until loaves are browned and sound hollow when tapped. Remove from the oven and the pans, and cool the loaves on their sides on a rack. Makes 2 medium-size loaves.

Notes on bread-making: Have all ingredients at room temperature before starting. Measure oil first, and then use the same spoon for the honey—the honey will then slip right off with no sticky mess. The amount of flour to use is always variable, depending on the type of flour, the weather, the altitude, etc.; develop a "feel" for what is right. Stir and knead vigorously; this spreads the yeast and develops the gluten, making light and evenly rising loaves. Try using coffee cans for bread pans—they make a nice shape for sandwiches; but take care to fill them only half full with dough. Cool loaves on their sides on a cake rack; this will help keep them from being bottom heavy.

WHOLE WHEAT PASTRY FLOUR Whole wheat pastry flour is made from soft winter wheat. Because it is lower in gluten than flour derived from hard wheat, it makes cakes and pastries that are tender and finely textured. If you are unable to locate whole wheat pastry flour, sift regular whole wheat flour a half-dozen times through a fine mesh sifter, reserving the bran that will not pass through for bread making. Also, make certain not to overbeat the batter (this will keep the gluten from developing and will give a tenderer cake), and add 1 teaspoon more baking powder than is called for in the recipe.

Whole wheat pastry flour can be substituted cup for cup in any recipe calling for white pastry or all-purpose flour. For a lighter cake, add ½ to 1 teaspoon more of baking powder. Whole wheat pastry flour can be mixed with regular whole wheat flour to make bread, but if used alone the result will be a very heavy loaf because of the lower gluten of this flour.

YARROW TEA This familiar roadside herb (*Achillea millefolia*) is also known as milfoil because of the many fine divisions of its leaves. Although yarrow was long ago said to ward off evil spirits, today it is primarily used to stimulate the appetite and to alleviate colitis symptoms. Tea can be made from either the fresh or dried leaves and flowers. It is astringent and can be used externally to treat oily skin and hair.

YEAST, BAKING Baking yeast is a living plant. Given a warm and moist environment, the yeast cells start to grow, and it is this growth that causes bread to rise. If the temperature is too cold or too hot, the yeast will not function; this is why all ingredients involved in bread-making must be lukewarm or at room temperature, and why rising must take place in a warm spot, and why the loaf stops rising soon after being placed in a hot oven.

Yeast is available commercially in two forms: dry or compressed. Dry yeast will keep for about six months. Compressed yeast is extremely perishable and should be used within a week, although it can be frozen successfully for longer periods of time. When its light gray color turns to brown, it is too old to use. More and more commercial baking yeasts contain BHT (butylated hydroxytoluene), a petroleum-base antioxidant that is best avoided. Examine labels for this ingredient; health food stores sell yeast without it.

YEAST, BREWER'S See *Brewer's Yeast*.

YERBA MATE TEA This tea is the national drink in many parts of South America and is made from the dried leaves of the maté evergreen tree. It has been used since time immemorial by the South American Indians (maté is the Inca word for the gourdlike vessel originally used to hold the beverage) and quickly picked up by the invading Portuguese and

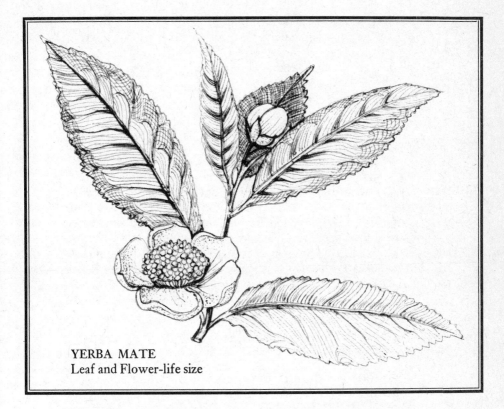

YERBA MATE
Leaf and Flower-life size

Spaniards who added "yerba" (meaning "herb") to its name. It is a stimulating and nourishing tea and is preferred by some to Oriental tea because of its purportedly lower caffeine content. Use 1 tablespoon maté to 2 cups boiling water; steep for 3 to 5 minutes, strain, and serve.

YERBA SANTA TEA This "holy herb" tea grows in California and was long used by the West Coast Indians to alleviate bronchial problems such as asthma, laryngitis, and hay fever. Its aromatic flavor and medicinal effects are still appreciated by herbal tea drinkers. The Indians at times smoked Yerba Santa leaves instead of tobacco . . . Sounds like a pleasant cure for smoker's cough!

YOGURT Yogurt is a cultured milk product that is custardlike in consistency and sour in taste. It has been enjoyed for thousands of years by Eastern Europeans and is at last coming into its own in this country. Its health benefits are so numerous as to be almost legendary. This is the item that produces all those centenarians in far-off Hunza villages, so they say. There is certainly no doubt that yogurt is very rich in B vitamins and calcium, and because of its high count of healthy bacteria is extremely useful in conditioning the intestinal tract. It soothes stomach ulcers, regulates the bowels in cases of constipation or diarrhea, is far easier to digest than milk, and helps repair the damage that antibiotics wreak upon the intestinal tract. It is also a delicious and extremely versatile food that can be used for breakfast, lunch, or dinner, as dessert, beverage, sauce, soup, or garnish.

Commercial yogurts may contain jelling agents, artificial flavoring and coloring, preservatives, and lots of sugar. Particularly avoid the flavored types; they are easily made at home using more healthful ingredients. Usually the yogurt carried in health food stores is dependably additive free. But you can save yourself a lot of money by making your own yogurt at home. It is very simple to do, and especially delicious to taste.

HOMEMADE YOGURT

1 qt. milk (raw, homogenized, skimmed, dried noninstant, evaporated, cow or goat)

3 tbsp. noninstant dried milk (optional, gives a firmer yogurt)

3 tbsp. unflavored yogurt (or a dry yogurt culture)

Jars with tops

Put the milk into a heavy pot and place over low heat. If you choose to add the dry milk, mix it into a smooth paste with a small amount of milk and stir it into the rest of the milk. Scald the milk; it should be steaming hot but not boiling. Remove from heat and let it cool to about 110 degrees (lukewarm) on a candy thermometer or until you can hold your finger in it for 10 seconds without burning. Cooling can be hastened by setting the pot of hot milk in a sink of cold water.

When the milk has cooled to the proper temperature, mix in the fresh yogurt or yogurt culture, making sure there are no lumps. Then ladle the mixture into clean jars and cap them.

The point now is to keep the yogurt at about 110 degrees for 3 to 8 hours. And here is where variety of approach creeps in. You can put the yogurt-filled bottles in a heavy pot with a few inches of warm water in it and set it over a pilot light, or on a warm (*not hot*) radiator, or in an oven that is warmed by a pilot light or turned on periodically to keep the atmosphere at about 110 degrees. Or put the jars in an electric frying pan shallowly filled with water and keep it at the lowest heat adjustment. In all cases, check the water temperature occasionally (with a thermometer or the 10-count finger test). If it is too cold the yogurt will not jell, and if it is too hot the yogurt bacteria will die and the milk will curdle.

Yogurt made with fresh yogurt as culture usually takes 3 to 5 hours to jell; made with dried yogurt culture, it takes longer—up to 8 hours. When the yogurt is ready (test by tipping a jar slightly or inserting a knife to test its firmness—the yogurt will become more firm with refrigeration), remove from the water and refrigerate. Enjoy yogurt plain, or sweetened with honey or maple syrup. Flavor it with jam or fresh fruit. For vanilla or coffee flavor, add vanilla extract or instant coffee with a little honey.

CURRIED EGGPLANT WITH YOGURT

1 eggplant, medium size   *2 tsp. ground coriander*
  (1–2 pounds)   *2–3 tsp. curry powder*
1 medium onion, chopped   *1 tbsp. tomato paste*
5 tbsp. vegetable oil   *1 tsp. salt*
  (preferably pressed   *1 c. yogurt*
  oil)

Slash the eggplant in several places with a knife, and bake in a 400-degree oven for 25 to 35 minutes or until tender. Cool the eggplant; then peel and chop it coarsely. In a skillet, sauté the chopped onion in the oil. When it is tender but not brown, add the coriander and curry powder (using a lesser amount if your curry powder is very strong, and more if it is mild), and cook for a couple of minutes. Stir in the tomato paste. Then add the eggplant and salt and simmer, while stirring, for 5 minutes. Spoon into a bowl, stir in the yogurt, and refrigerate. Serve chilled as an appetizer or as an accompaniment to a main course of curry.

Serves four to six.

YOGURT BREAKFAST

2 c. yogurt
2 oranges, peeled and
chopped
1 apple, chopped

½ c. nuts, chopped
3 tbsp. raisins
6 tbsp. wheat germ
2 tbsp. honey

Mix all ingredients together and serve immediately.

Serves three to four.

SUBJECT INDEX

RECIPE INDEX